A SERVICE FOR THE PEOPLE

A SERVICE FOR THE PEOPLE

RICK MEHTA
Cognitive Psychologist & Defender of Truth

Foreword by Scott D. G. Ventureyra
Editor-in-Chief at True Freedom Press

True Freedom Press

TRUE FREEDOM PRESS

A SERVICE FOR THE PEOPLE

Edited by Scott D. G. Ventureyra

First published in Ottawa, Ontario, Canada
in 2023 by True Freedom Press.
https://www.scottventureyra.com/true-freedom-press
truefreedompress@gmail.com

PAPERBACK ISBN: 978-1-998917-00-6
EBOOK ISBN: 978-1-998917-01-3

Disclaimer Notice

Contents

Foreword

Dr. Rick Mehta's book is the first instalment by a sole author (other than my own) to be published by True Freedom Press. My decision to publish this book had nothing to do with whether I agreed or disagreed with Mehta, but instead had to do with his ability to think freely and unapologetically. To paraphrase a quote commonly attributed to 18th-century French enlightenment philosopher François-Marie Arouet, most commonly known as Voltaire, gets to the essence of what True Freedom Press is all about: "I may not agree with what you say, but I will defend to the death your right to say it."[1] This is precisely the reason I founded True Freedom Press in late 2020, namely, to publish works that other presses refuse to publish. Even Christian publishing houses would rather appease the world than publish works that defend truth and God. Publishing books like these embodies the spirit of True Freedom Press, a press that defends the pursuit of truth regardless of how uncomfortable, unpopular, or unsavoury it may be to many.

True Freedom Press promotes free speech and freedom of expression. With the pervasiveness of censorship throughout the legacy media, Big Tech platforms such as Facebook, Twitter, Instagram, Google, and others,

1 This quote originates with Voltaire's biographer, Evelyn Beatrice Hall. She wrote this in *The Friends of Voltaire* in order to show readers what Voltaire's overall attitude was on the issue of freedom of speech. See Evelyn Beatrice Hall, *The Friends of Voltaire* (New York: Putnam's, 1906), 199.

university campuses, work settings, publishing houses, and even places of worship, true freethinkers are increasingly seeking alternative platforms and methods of communication. True Freedom Press offers an alternative to this Orwellian nightmare that has become so commonplace throughout Western consciousness. It is an avenue for conservatives, theists, libertarians, free-thinkers, and others to express their positions in an open and honest fashion without fear of being stifled by political correctness. Little do many realize that political correctness is an oppressive tool to prevent dissenting views. The term itself originated with Leon Trotsky and was used by genocidal tyrants like Mao Zedong. Over the past 20 years, we have seen a dramatic increase in the censorship of unpopular ideas that counter certain narratives, such as woke ideologies, and in the past three years, anything that counters the single narrative of COVID-19.

True Freedom Press upholds a traditional understanding of tolerance, one that defends an individual's right to hold a particular position and express it freely even if it offends others. To write freely is to have the ability to offend. The truth may offend at first, but it should be embraced for the sake of authentic living and expression.

In an age where postmodernism and relativism (both metaphysical and moral) run rampant throughout our educational institutions, from junior kindergarten to the post-doctoral level, the denial of objective truth is at every turn, no matter how incoherent such a concept is. The reality of the situation is that, if you deny the truth, you affirm it through its denial. There is no escaping this fact. Aristotle stated this very succinctly: "To say of what is that it is not, or of what is not that it is, is false, while to say of what is that it is, and of what is not that it is not, is true."[2] This is why conversing with those who can't even agree on whether objective truth exists or not is so difficult. For postmodernists and critical theorists, truth is merely subjective, and they see the world as a power struggle between two groups: those who oppress and those who are oppressed. For better or worse, a Christian would have a more fruitful discussion with a traditional atheist than with a postmodern-woke inclined Christian (as contradictory as that sounds), because both agree that an objective truth exists to be discovered. Without the existence of truth, all intellectual endeavours would dissolve, rendering any form of communication impossible.

Whether one likes it or not, the truth exists, and we can come to know it. Our education system and culture presuppose that truth is either relative or at best solely verifiable through the scientific method, but this is mistaken. Truth is indeed discernible through the tools of mathematics, logic, and science, but it can also be known through innate knowledge, faith, experience, and intuition. Nevertheless, it is inescapable that the human experience is permeated with many beliefs that cannot be proven or disproven, including belief in the external physical world, our own minds, other minds, the intelligibility of the world, and that the past was not suddenly created with the appearance of age. Such beliefs have been deemed self-evident axioms (or properly basic beliefs) by some Christian philosophers, such as Alvin

2 Aristotle, *Metaphysics*, 1011b25.

Plantinga and William Alston. So, even though such views cannot be "proven" scientifically or rationally, they are nevertheless true, and we are justified in believing them. Since the 1960s, there has been a revival in studying the objective truth of Christian theism. Arguments for God's existence have had a strong revival with thinkers such as Stuart Hackett, Richard Swinburne, Dallas Willard, William Lane Craig, and J.P. Moreland. This is in part due to the collapse of verificationism, which suggested that for a sentence to have meaning it should be empirically verifiable, i.e., by the five senses, and therefore that knowledge of God was impossible and statements about God meaningless. The interesting thing about the verification principle is that it was revealed to be incoherent itself, by its very criteria, since it could not be verified by the senses. There are also moral truths that we all know innately, such as that it is morally abhorrent and objectively wrong to torture little babies for fun. Certainly, objective moral values and duties do exist, and they are transpersonal and not dictated by consensus, trends in culture, or how we have evolved socio-biologically. What's more is that in Christianity, truth is a person and much more than an abstract concept; it's relational. Nevertheless, whether it be scientific truths, theological truths, or truth as in the person of Jesus of Nazareth (John 1:14–15), who was vindicated by God for his radical claims of divine self-understanding (Dan 7; Matt. 11:5; 25:34–46), objective truth exists.

Mehta, unlike many of his former colleagues at Acadia University and throughout Western academia, who are stuck in a postmodernist mindset, upholds the existence of truth and believes that we can come to know it. Moreover, Mehta notes the importance of discussion, debate, and disagreement since sometimes the truth is not easy to discern. There needs to be a feedback mechanism where we discard and refine our arguments as we come to acknowledge when they do not fully align with the evidence. The universities, on the other hand, have become cult-like, whereby social justice trumps someone's competence as a researcher and instructor, and therefore the longstanding protections of tenured professorships. Freedom is subordinated to the ideologies of social justice radicals who dictate what is correct and incorrect thinking. It is truly Orwellian in nature. This is precisely what we see now with the recent absurd re-education demands made by the College of Psychologists of Ontario of Jordan Peterson that seem more like fetishized punishments than having anything to do with reality.

Aside from living in an era of truth denial, or post-truth, and apathy, we live in a period of great cowardice. Although many people realize something is tremendously wrong with the COVID narrative, for instance, they fear speaking out due to potential repercussions. These people would rather do what is expedient than what is right. They would rather "follow orders" and comply with whatever government mandates are in place in order to not suffer from any inconveniences or consequences. This group of people is known as "bystanders." They claim no involvement, but these are precisely the people who have allowed great evils to transpire throughout history. We needn't look too far back to find examples. Historically, "bystanders" can be considered complicit in the atrocities perpetrated by the Nazis, Soviets, and Maoists since they did nothing to prevent them. We got a taste of this as vaccinated friends and family stood looking on as the vaccine-free individuals were punished for deciding not to receive the jab. Even worse, some people, including family members, demonized and shunned the vaccine-free, for which there was no scientific or ethical justification whatsoever. As time passes, more and more evidence accumulates to support the wise decision to remain vaccine-free. (I argue this and much more in my co-authored and edited volume, *COVID-19: A Dystopian Delusion*.) Collectively, "the people" are far stronger than tyrants and their minions. Mehta is definitely not a coward, and he follows his convictions to the end. In fact, he has shown great courage in taking the uncomfortable stances he has. Mehta is a legitimate defender of truth; he has the courage, strength, and conviction to defend what he believes to be epistemically warranted and morally true.

Regrettably, Mehta has been dismissed and, in some cases, ignored by legal authorities, his former colleagues, fellow Christians, the police (including the RCMP), and others, but this is a grave mistake on their part. Sometimes we ignore the very issues that we are afraid to confront or do not know how to adequately respond to. That way, you can hope the problem goes away, but Mehta will not be going away any time soon. Mehta has something important to say, whether we agree with him or not, and perhaps if one listens closely, there is something they can learn that will help them see things from a perspective they had not considered and even further, to discover a world that would otherwise be hidden to them. Mehta is a dangerous man. He's dangerous because he speaks the truth to power (as his conscience and beliefs dictate) without reservation. Those who ignore Mehta will do so at their own peril. Although one may not agree with any of what Mehta argues, he is careful and meticulous in his documentation and analysis of our corrupted governments, courts, medical institutions (even animal hospitals!), and academic institutions, and he provides reasoned arguments and evidence to support his position. His style is entertaining and engaging, and even comical at times, but most importantly, we must pay close attention to the substance of his claims and verify them for ourselves.

Lastly, Mehta boldly speaks of Satan (the greatest deceiver of the world), something that does not resonate well with modern ears, including those influenced by postmodernism. As unpalatable and superstitious as the spiritual dimension and the demonic may sound to many twenty-first century ears, it is the best way to understand the world's situation. I have struggled with accepting this reality for quite some time and have regarded it as irrational, remaining agnostic to the existence of demons and Satan. But I have found that this reality in opposition to God makes the most sense of my internal struggles, the struggles of humanity, and the struggle between good and evil. Given a theological backdrop, there is no other way to understand our inner darkness and the outer darkness of the world.

The devil hides in plain sight, and he has convinced many that he doesn't exist. Mehta, through his experience, shows us that we mustn't fall into Satan's trap. It is worth mentioning that there are two dangers when thinking about the demonic realm. First is its dismissal; the demonic realm is one that must not be dismissed since it is very real, as a deceased childhood friend recently told me in an eerie dream, "The devil is real." I took these words as a sort of cautionary advice about an imminent danger, one that we easily ignore in the spatiotemporal reality we inhabit as body-soul composite beings. It is indeed a reality, even though it belongs to an invisible spiritual realm. Second, it should not consume one's thoughts because fixation on the demonic has consequences. Neither of these extremes are healthy. So, while Satan does exist and wreaks havoc on our souls, the Creator and Redeemer of all has defeated sin and evil on the Cross. Without God, there is no devil. Similarly, without good, there is no evil since evil functions as a privation of the good; otherwise, as the famous zoologist Richard Dawkins states, we are left with "at bottom, no design, no purpose, no evil, no good, nothing but pitiless indifference."[3] The sacred Scriptures make it clear that Satan mixes the truth with lies, something that Mehta recognizes and sees through the vast corruption throughout our broken institutions. Thus, those who are not awake to the times and who do not follow the inner witness of the Holy Spirit are subject to falling prey to the false narratives of COVID-19, woke culture, and the denial of objective truth, as exemplified by postmodernism. Nevertheless, rest assured that it is all part of God's plan. Therefore, "be alert and of sober mind. Your enemy the devil prowls around like a roaring lion looking for someone to devour. Resist him, standing firm in the faith, because you know that the family of believers throughout the world is undergoing the same kind of sufferings" (1 Peter 5:8–13).

Now, read on and witness how Mehta, in his capacity as a cognitive and behavioral psychologist, unravels the corruption embedded within many of Canada's broken institutions. The material contained in this book is indeed a service for the people.

Scott D. G. Ventureyra, PhD
Editor-in-Chief at True Freedom Press
Author and editor of *COVID-19: A Dystopian Delusion*
Ottawa, Canada
January 2023

3 Richard Dawkins, *River out of Eden: A Darwinian View of Life* (New York: Basic Books, 1995), 133.

Preface

In order for you — the reader — to understand this book, it is important that you understand the context in which you are reading it and the characteristics about me that make me unique as a human being. I will start with the context in which you are reading this book.

If you have read Sir John Glubb's seminal work *The Fate of Empires and The Search for Survival* (1976) and have observed the world around you objectively, then you would realize that our civilization has been living in the Age of Decadence, with its hallmarks being materialism and a loss of the sense of duty that resides in societies that hold themselves accountable to a deity, and that the Age of Decadence precedes a civilization's downfall. In other words, we are living in a civilization that is collapsing due to the weight of its hubris.

Turning to the characteristics about me that speak to my uniqueness, I will first describe my well-rounded academic background and then speak to how this has served the public's interests. My undergraduate degree was in neuroscience because I was interested in understanding the biological foundations of human behaviour. My Master's degree was in psychopharmacology (an area of neuroscience) because I was interested in learning how drugs affect brain functioning and behaviour. Finally, my doctorate degree and postdoctoral training were in associative learning because of its implications for judgement and decision making; the question of interest in this research had to do with the mechanism by which people learn to associate — for example — blue skies with sunshine and gray skies with rain. While I was an academic, I shifted the focus of my research from associative learning (a narrow area of research in psychology) to judgement and decision making (a broad area of research in psychology).

I was a professor of psychology at Acadia University between July 1, 2003, and August 31, 2018. The Department of Psychology at Acadia University initially hired me to teach the department's courses on the biological foundations of behaviour. Interestingly, enrollment in these courses increased once I started teaching them. Indeed, the interest became so strong that the department increased its course offerings in this area and established a neuroscience option for its undergraduates. Furthermore, the department attributed this success to my ability to make intimidating material accessible to students from all walks of life.

As further evidence for my success as a teacher, I will mention that I was the recipient of two teaching awards in the 2016 —2017 academic year: one in February 2017 and one in April 2017. As an aside, I will also mention that Dr. Peter J. Ricketts's tenure as president of Acadia University started on July 1, 2017, and that he terminated my employment at the university without cause (in the absence of professional misconduct on my part) on August 31, 2018, and then defamed me on October 30, 2019, i.e., well after my employment dispute with the university was settled on April 1, 2019.

In order for students with no biological background to understand the course content that I was covering, I needed to first have a solid understanding of how the various parts of the brain work in isolation. The standard to which I held myself was what I called "the grandmother rule," i.e., my grandmother (if she were alive and could speak English) could attend my classes and understand the course content that I was covering because I was articulating myself clearly. After understanding the function of various brain parts in isolation, I needed to understand how the various parts of the brain worked together as a system. Finally, I needed to understand what would happen if one or more parts of the brain system I was describing failed to function properly, as well as the consequences of this failure on human behavior.

This ability served the public's interests when I later needed to learn how our legal system works. Given my success in making biological concepts accessible to students who had no biological background, it was not a stretch for me to learn how individual pieces of legislation work in isolation, how various pieces of legislation work together as part of a legal system, and what happens to human behaviour when one or more pieces of legislation are not designed to serve the public's interests. Unfortunately, most people do not understand that human behaviour is often situation-dependent. Thus, if one or more unscrupulous individuals wish to control the behaviour of a population, all that person or group needs to do is manipulate the situation by enacting laws that are not in the best interests of the public (e.g., implement legislation that ignores issues such as conflict of interest), and chaos will inevitably ensue.

While my biological background is one of the characteristics that make me unique, another characteristic is that I may well be the only academic in Canada who also has a background in the narrow area of associative learning. This background has served the public's interests because, if I understand that superstitious behaviours arise due to people making false associations, e.g., associating a rabbit's foot with success, then it is not a stretch for me to also understand that people who make false associations are at risk for having faulty belief systems in which the thoughts that are in a person's mind are not associated logically with other ideas that are in that person's mind.

If the ideas that are in a person's mind are not connected logically to one another, then it should be no surprise if that person's speech is disjointed or hard to follow given that language is connected to thought and decision making – which makes conversations difficult if not outright impossible. As well, it should be no surprise that it is easy for that person to be duped because that person cannot discern truth from lies or fact from fiction, e.g., people who advocate for healthy living but then agree to get injected with an experimental drug without informed consent. This problem becomes even more pronounced when the society in which one lives is filled with people who have muddled minds. I say this not as a personal attack, but rather in the spirit of a psychologist who is explaining to a patient why he or she is having problems in their life and the impact of these problems on other people.

The final characteristic that I will describe that sets me apart from most Canadian academics is that I am a follower of Jesus Christ. In the early part of my life, I was an atheist. I later decided to become an agnostic because I thought it was arrogant of me to say that God does not exist given how difficult it is to prove a negative in science. Thus, for much of my career as an academic, I took the position that the question of whether or not God exists is a worthwhile one to ask but that science is not equipped to answer this question. My approach was very similar to that of Doubting Thomas's skepticism when he was told that Jesus Christ had risen from the dead, i.e., "if I see it, I will believe it" or, to borrow a famous line from the movie *Jerry Maguire,* "show me the resurrection." Because of these parallels, I have a deeper understanding than most people of what Jesus Christ meant when he told Thomas words to the effect "You see and therefore you believe, but think of how much more blessed are the people who have never seen me yet believe in me."[4]

4 **Editor's note***: It may come as a surprise to many, but the historicity of the resurrection of Jesus has quite a solid foundation. There are many works that provide credible historical evidence for the resurrection of Jesus and other central claims of the Christian faith. I would recommend two books: one is a popular level book titled *The New Evidence That Demands A Verdict* (2019), written by Christian apologists Josh McDowell and Sean McDowell, and the other is *The Resurrection of Jesus: A New Historiographical Approach* (2010), written by the New Testament scholar Michael R. Licona. It is important to realize that Christianity has a rich intellectual foundation. Christianity is not in opposition to science and reason. For instance, assumptions regarding the intelligibility and rationality of reality shaped much of the empiricism in science, as well as the use of mathematics to describe natural processes. Indeed, theological insights and understanding inspired developments in modern scientific thought. This is especially true of great scientific minds such as Isaac Newton, Johannes Kepler, René Descartes, Galileo Galilei, and Nicolas Copernicus, who posited that the structure of physical reality was knowable. These explicitly theological ideas—according to which there is intelligibility and comprehensibility in reality because of God's role as Creator—inspired scientists to adopt a type of reverse engineering mode of thinking (whereby humans could possibly even modify and perfect creation) in order to understand how things were created (this was precisely the mode of thinking practiced by Isaac Newton). This, in my estimation, does not take away from one's faith but deepens it.

After going through much turmoil in both my personal and professional lives over the course of July 25, 2017, to October 30, 2018, I decided to turn my life over to Jesus Christ in February 2019. Interestingly, I made this decision roughly one year before COVID-19 became a household name. I credit my faith in Jesus Christ for allowing me to not only fight for the public's interests in my capacity as a dedicated public servant, but to also reach a successful conclusion to this battle on January 3, 2023. My hope in writing this book is that the readers who are lost but have eyes to see and ears to hear will come to believe and will therefore be saved.

In my opinion, a characteristic that sets me apart from Christians and helps to explain my success is that my faith is like yeast that has permeated its way through a pizza's dough whereas many Christians' faith is like a pizza's topping in the sense that it is easy to move or remove a slice of pepperoni or pineapple because it is not fixed to the pizza, e.g., it is easy for a feminist to ignore the sections of the Bible that they would describe as "oppressive" due to "patriarchy." I mean this in the sense that my impression is that my spiritual beliefs are integrated into my system of beliefs, whereas many Christians compartmentalize their faith from their other beliefs; this would explain why so many Christians have faith in or idolize political leaders or lawyers — or would vote for an adulterer or philanderer. In other words, they fail to see that the lesser of evils is still an evil.

I realize that the previous paragraph may not be accessible to many people and that I may be coming across as arrogant. To address this issue, I will explain my point in a different way. When the Bible makes reference to humanity's "sinful nature," I interpret that text as meaning that God is referring to the way in which the human brain is organized and how it develops from the fetal to adult stages of development, as well as the kinds of information that people fill their brains with over the course of their lives. I also interpret the notion of "sinful nature" as referring to two major weaknesses that all humans have in common and need to overcome if we are to grow: self-deception and lack of awareness of how other people see us, i.e., the impression that we are making on other people.[5] I believe that the Bible's notion of people's "sinful nature" helps to explain humanity's quirks, e.g., the person who goes to great lengths to watch the food they eat so that their body is healthy, yet consumes information that is akin to junk food that poisons that person's mind.

Outside of academia, my interests in books and movies have included murder mysteries and whodunnits, e.g., detective stories written by Agatha Christie or Sir Arthur Conan Doyle. I have also long been a fan of legal dramas and books or movies about crime, e.g., movies such as *The Untouchables* or *A Few Good Men*, and have fantasized about writing a courtroom drama. That opportunity arose when all of my legal battles recently reached their logical conclusion, which brings us to the issue of how this book is organized.

This book consists of a main storyline that is contained in Section 1 ("Psychological Intervention in Two Court Cases"). The main storyline makes reference to events

5 In the case of Christians, this means that they are not asking themselves how Jesus Christ sees them.

that happened in the past; these events are described in each of the 10 tabs that are in Section 2 of this book. Thus, the idea is that the reader should read the contents of Tab 1 when the main storyline makes reference to Tab 1, the contents of Tab 2 when the main storyline makes reference to Tab 2, etc.

If this book were a movie, it would start with a psychologist — instead of a detective or lawyer — interrupting a court session to make a presentation in which he demonstrates that everyone in the courtroom and proceeding — i.e., the lawyers, judge, police officers, and jury – has an incorrect understanding of the facts of the case that is being heard. During the presentation, the facts of the case unfold in flashbacks. In the ideal circumstance, the presentation blows away not only the other characters in the movie but also the audience.

Rather than give away any spoilers about the book, I will close this preface by saying that I anticipate that this book will be a difficult read for many readers, in part because it will challenge many of their cherished beliefs and in part because truth can sometimes be stranger than fiction. But having one's beliefs challenged is essential for growth and may well be the best service that I can provide for the people.

As for acknowledgments, I would not have a story to tell unless God's invisible hand had been working in the background of my entire life. The only reason that I can fathom for why God did this for me when I did not believe in Him is that my mum prayed for me daily while she was alive and taught me the importance of responsibility; in my view, raising a child to become a responsible adult is synonymous with teaching a child to live a life of "repentance." For these and other reasons, I am dedicating this book to her (Kanta Mehta, April 25, 1938 – October 11, 2018).

I would like to close this preface by thanking Dr. Scott Ventureyra for not only providing me with a platform by which I can communicate with the people whose interests I am trying to serve, but also for his editorial feedback and moral support. My hope in writing this book is that it will make a meaningful difference in our civil discourse.

Rick Mehta, PhD
Coldbrook, Nova Scotia
January 2023

SECTION 1

PSYCHOLOGICAL INTERVENTION IN TWO COURT CASES

(January 3, 2023)

1535 Meghan Drive
Coldbrook, NS
B4R 1A1

January 3, 2023

Dartmouth Provincial Courthouse
277 Pleasant Street
Dartmouth, NS
B2Y 4B7

Psychological Intervention in Two Court Cases:

1) King Charles[6] vs. Morgan May Guptill and Jeremy MacKenzie

2) King Charles vs. Weston Christian Fellowship[7] and Marty Elson (KEN No.: 8513762, 8513748, 8513749)

Dear Dartmouth Provincial Courthouse et al.,

I am writing to you regarding two separate but related cases that are before Nova Scotia's courts.

6 Although I may not have used the correct terminology, I am sure that all parties know the cases to which I am referring.

7 This church received roughly $100K in fines in May 2021 for holding their services despite an injunction order that was passed by the Government of Nova Scotia that banned churches from holding

When one case has implications for another case, then logic dictates that the two cases be consolidated in order for justice to be served. For this reason, I have consolidated the two cases that are in the subject heading. I note that one of these cases is before the provincial court in Dartmouth and that the other case is before the provincial court in Kentville; I also note that I have addressed this psychological intervention to the courthouse in Dartmouth and that I am copying the following parties on this psychological intervention:

- provincial court in Kentville,
- the Crown Attorney's Office in Kentville,
- the Crown Attorney's Office in Dartmouth,
- counsel for Weston Christian Fellowship and Elder Elson,
- Elder Elson, and
- Morgan May Guptill[8]

---

their services because they were classified as "gatherings". My understanding is that Weston Christian Fellowship is the only church in Nova Scotia that defied the injunction order. On October 20, 2021, Rebel News posted an interview of Sheila Gunn Reid with the church's elders and the church's counsel. I came across this video and the church's Facebook page (which appears to be hosted by an American group that calls itself Carpe Fide) in December 2021, and this is what made me decide to attend the church's services. I did not include this information in my submission to the court, but thought that I should include these facts in this book. Another point of fact that I will mention is that I submitted my Statement of Claim to challenge the constitutionality of the *Health Protection Act* order (legislation passed by the Government of Nova Scotia) in May 2021.

8 Because I do not have Ms. Guptill's mailing address, I am sending this document to her by email. And because I have no connection with Mr. MacKenzie, I will ask Ms. Guptill to forward this document to Mr. MacKenzie.

To expedite the process, I am sending all of the parties their copy of this psychological intervention directly via Xpresspost instead of mailing all of the copies to the court to get a court-stamp before mailing the parties their copy of this psychological intervention.

The impetus for this psychological intervention stems from correspondence that I sent to the provincial court in Dartmouth by registered mail that is dated December 13, 2022; I will make reference to this correspondence later in this document.

Introduction

Under normal or ordinary circumstances, I would not write to a court in my capacity as a cognitive psychologist; but these are not normal or ordinary circumstances. As evidence that we are not living under ordinary circumstances, I will point out that COVID-19 appeared on the scene in the year 2020 and that an objective examination of the symbolism underlying the year 2020 reveals that the symbol "2020" can also be depicted as "20/20", which stands for "perfect acuity or clarity". Thus, from a Biblical perspective, "2020" symbolizes the year in which all would eventually become clear or be revealed in the sense that everything that was hidden in the dark will eventually come to light, i.e., Book of Revelation. We clearly are living in extraordinary times.

Another piece of the puzzle is that, before the fall of the Roman Empire, the apostle Paul wrote "For this lawlessness is already at work secretly, and it will remain secret until the one who is holding it back steps out of the way" (2 Thessalonians 2: 7; NLT).[9] Paul's statement tells us that the events of today can be traced back to events that transpired before the fall of the Roman Empire (roughly 50 AD) and that we are dealing with the cumulative effect of all of these events. The short version of a long story is that we now live in an age of postmodernism, i.e., the view that there is no objective truth, and that postmodernism in turn explains why we now live in an age of mass psychosis is which mental illness is the norm.

To establish my credibility, I will point out that while I may not be a lawyer, I have expertise in judgment and decision making that I expect the court and other parties to recognize; indeed, my expertise justifies me intervening in the court's affairs for the purpose of serving the public's interests. As evidence for the fact that the court has recognized my academic credentials, I will point out that Justice Hunt referred to me as "Dr. Mehta" in his decision against me (KEN No. 506242) and that Justice Smith referred to me as "Dr. Mehta" in her decision against me (KEN No. 506256). If these Justices were willing to recognize my academic credentials, then I was being reasonable when I also expected them to recognize the expertise in judgement and decision making that came with my academic credentials. By failing to recognize my expertise, Justices Hunt and Smith made decisions that were not in the public's interests. Thus, my act of intervening in these two court cases has nothing to do with a personal vendetta but instead has to do with me serving a greater good.

9 While the King James Version (KJV) of the Bible is the version that people swear on in Canada's courts, the wording of this verse that is in the New Living Translation provides us with insight into current world affairs.

An interesting point of fact about me is that I have been compared to Dr. Jordan B. Peterson. In case anyone thinks that I have any association with this talking head, I hope that the following screenshot of a tweet that I sent on December 19, 2022, will demonstrate that I am not associated with him in any way, shape or form because I am a serious academic:

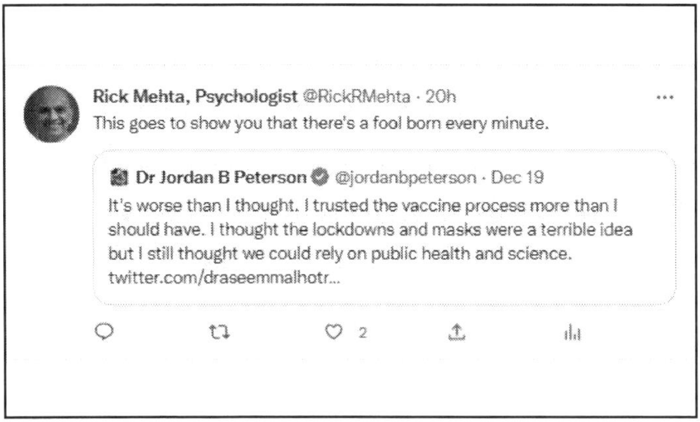

I hope that everyone sees the humour in Dr. Peterson "trusting the vaccine process", thinking that "we could rely on public health", and thinking that public health's policies were based on "science".

Legal Background

To understand how we got into this mess, one needs to understand that Satan – who was a liar from the start – is the god[10] of this world and that this fact in turn explains

10 Please note that I used a small g instead of the capitalized version of this letter, i.e., "god" instead of "God".

why our courts have Satanic origins. As one example that demonstrates that Canada's legal system has Satanic origins, I will point out that "Black's Law Dictionary" – a book in which words have definitions that are different from the definitions used in everyday language – is the foundation of Canada's legal system. Black's Law Dictionary implicates Satan because deception (lying) is the only plausible reason why our legal system would define terms in a manner that is different from how terms are used in everyday language and are properly understood.

The natural consequence of Canada's courts having Satanic origins is that our courts and legal system are in contravention of the "supremacy of God"[11] that both the *Canadian Bill of Rights* and the *Canadian Charter of Rights and Freedoms* cite as prerequisite to "rule of law" in a free society. In my capacity as a Christian, I have a duty to use the gifts that God has given me to remedy this problem.

To understand how I plan to get Canada out of this mess, one needs to understand two key points in Canadian history. The first point is that the *Canadian Charter of Rights and Freedoms* – which was assented into law in 1981 – is a political document that was designed for corrupt courts to abuse; from a Justice's perspective, the *Canadian Charter of Rights and Freedoms* reduced Canada's laws to "Do what thou wilt", which is often referred to as Satan's motto given this saying has links to the occult, e.g., the writings of Aleister Crowley or Anton LaVey. The second – and more interesting point – is that the Government of Nova Scotia passed three (3) pieces of

11 Because the letter "g" is capitalized, it is referring to the God described in the Bible because He is a true and living God.

legislation in 1989 – two of which were corrupt and one of which was not corrupt:

1) Nova Scotia Trade Union Act (corrupt legislation),
2) Nova Scotia Human Rights Act (corrupt legislation), and
3) Nova Scotia Defamation Act (non-corrupt legislation).

From a Biblical perspective, this second point is particularly interesting because the Satanists who run this province unintentionally passed a piece of legislation (Nova Scotia Defamation Act) that has origins that are holy and could therefore be used by a Christian as a mustard seed to make a web of deceit fold on itself.

To understand why the Nova Scotia Defamation Act has origins that are holy, one first needs to understand the legal definition of defamation, which can be summarized as "false statements about a person that have been disseminated to at least one third party"; this definition is consistent with violating the Commandment that says "Thou shalt not bear false witness against thy neighbour (Exodus 20:13; KJV)". Next, one needs to consider the most compelling defence to defamation: truth; that is because Jesus Christ tells us that He IS the truth, i.e., "I am the way, the truth, and the life (John 14:6; KJV)".

From a Biblical perspective, by passing the Nova Scotia Defamation Act, the provincial government set up a situation for our courts that is akin to the situation that Adam and Even faced with the Tree of Knowledge that was in the Garden of Eden. In the same way that God disclosed to Adam and Eve that they should not mess with the Tree of Knowledge, Satan should have disclosed to Justice Smith that it is a bad idea to lie in a defamation lawsuit, especially when the plaintiff and defendants in that lawsuit already agreed that Canada's legal system is corrupt and this fact in turn explained why President Ricketts decided to be naughty on October 30, 2019, i.e., well after my employment dispute with Acadia University and the Acadia University Faculty Association – which transpired under the Nova Scotia Trade Union Act – was settled on April 1, 2019.

Because the concept of naughtiness is of central importance in this psychological intervention, I will highlight that when I was a child, many of the children who were caught being naughty ended up getting a spanking on their bottoms or some other form of discipline that was given with love, e.g., a kick to their bottom, being grounded, etc.; for better or for worse, this was how many parents attempted to instill the children from my generation with a healthy fear of the Lord.[12] Fast forward to the present, I appreciate how discipline is far better than being on a path to hell. This explains my drive and the lengths that I am willing to go to save my fellow man from the fires of hell.

Chronology

In this section of this psychological intervention, I will list the following facts and documents in chronological order that the court needs to take into consideration in order to make a correct decision:

12 An obvious disadvantage of this approach is that many children, myself included, responded by trying to avoid getting caught instead of not being naughty.

1) I was a member of the congregation of Weston Christian Fellowship between late December 2021 and early July 2022. Below are four facts and observations that I made during the time that I was there:

    a. After one of the services, a member of the congregation who does not attend regularly asked me if I thought that Elder Elson rehashed the same message at every sermon. I responded by saying that listening to Elder Elson was like listening to a broken record.

    b. Elder Elson's wife disclosed to me that she is dyslexic and that she reads the same passages of the Bible over and over again in order to understand them. Her statement disclosed to me that she likely has not received treatment for her dyslexia and that she learns by using rote repetition (the least effective form of learning) instead of active learning, e.g., thinking about how the text that is being read can be applied to one's own life or to explain the world around them. This approach to information processing guarantees a superficial understanding of all subject matter.

    The combination of postmodernism and a superficial understanding of the Bible helps to explain why Elder Elson and his wife get into heated debates over the Bible in which their faces turn red and in which Elder Elson's veins pop out of his neck.

    c. I tried to raise my concerns in a diplomatic and respectful fashion with the elders while I was a member of the congregation at Weston Christian Fellowship, but unfortunately – and as noted by the philosopher Daniel Dennett – "There's simply no polite way to tell people that they've committed their life to an illusion."

d. If the congregation at Weston Christian Fellowship is filled with people who are oblivious to the fact that their church leaders are postmodernists who likely would perform poorly on tests of literacy[13], then it should be no surprise that the congregation is also oblivious to the fact that their leaders are in a state of psychosis, i.e., they are out of touch with reality. For this reason, this church should be approached as if it is a mental institution or insane asylum instead of a house of prayer. The fact that this church is one of the more theologically sound churches that I have encountered in this province since becoming a Christian in February 2019 speaks to the sad state of Nova Scotia's churches.

2) TAB 1 contains the body of the first affidavit that I swore to in my constitutional challenge of the *Health Protection Act* order (dated July 8, 2021). In this affidavit, I proved that Satan is the mastermind behind both social justice and COVID-19; I also linked Acadia University with both Prime Minister Justin Trudeau and Satan.

13 Literacy consists of reading comprehension and numeracy (ability to reason about numerical information) and plays an important role in judgement and decision making.

a. The first point of fact that I will highlight is that Justice Hunt based his decision solely on his reading of my Statement of Claim in this matter. In other words, his decision makes it clear that he never read this affidavit or the affidavit that I will reference later in this document, even though my two affidavits spoke to issues such as my qualifications and credibility.

b. The second point of fact is that the court never asked why Dr. Terry's clinic was being represented by Jonathan Cuming (TMC Law) instead of the clinic's Recognized Agent (Tim Hergett, Hergett Law). Had Mr. Hergett and the court done what was right (admit that the *Health Protection Act* order was unconstitutional), then the vaccine mandates would not have been implemented and there would have been no need for the Freedom Convoy. As well, people would probably not be "dying suddenly" at this time.

3) TAB 2 contains the body of the second affidavit that I swore to in my constitutional challenge of the *Health Protection Act* order (dated November 30, 2021).

4) On February 15, 2022, Justice Hunt published a decision in which he defamed me (KEN No. 506242).

5) TAB 3 contains a copy of the body of a letter that I sent to both the Kentville Crown Attorney's Office and New Minas Detachment of the Royal Canadian Mounted Police (RCMP) that was dated

March 8, 2022, pertaining to my concerns about the Supreme Court of Nova Scotia discriminating against me for not being mentally disabled. Unfortunately, I never received a response to this letter.

6) On March 14, 2022, Justice Smith published her decision in which she defamed me and in which she ordered me to pay $10K to Acadia University and $10K to the Acadia University Faculty Association, even though their lawyers lied in a court of law, i.e., perjury is a *Criminal Code* offense.

7) On March 23, 2022, the RCMP issued a press release written by Constable[14] Guillaume Tremblay in which the RCMP stated that they had arrested Ms. Morgan May Guptill and Mr. Jeremy MacKenzie for protesting outside of Dr. Robert Strang's home.

    a. I cringed when I found out about their arrests because my professional opinion is that these defendants need a spanking on their bottoms in order to address their idiocy, i.e., if one knows that they are dealing with opponents who are dishonest and have the law on their side, the last thing that that person should do is give their opponents something to work with. In addition, the Crown attorneys and the officers who made the arrests need a spanking on their bottoms; because the Crown answers to King Charles (a globalist and Satanist), King Charles needs a spanking on his bottom. Finally,

14 I note that this constable is now a corporal.

because the Provincial Court in Dartmouth did not throw out this case, the people at the court who are involved with this case need a spanking on their bottoms. In short, everyone associated with this case needs a spanking on their bottoms. But to paraphrase a famous line from "The Dark Knight", I am here to give people the spanking they need (a spanking that is given with love) instead of the spanking they deserve (a spanking that is given with hate or vengeance). I will return to the arrests of Ms. Guptill and Mr. MacKenzie later in this document.

b. I have commented on social media that the phenomenon known as mass psychosis (large scale mental illness) can be observed not only in people who have drank the COVID Kool-Aid, but also in people who have not. For example, I see no difference between these groups of people when it comes to issues such as posting selfies or posting an excessive number of pictures of oneself online; this conduct is a clear indicator of narcissism, which is a risk factor for psychosis. These facts explain why the symptoms of mass psychosis manifest themselves differently in the two groups of people and that, for now, the symptoms of mass psychosis are harder to detect in people who have not drank the COVID Kool-Aid.

8) TAB 4 contains the cover letter to a brief that I hand-delivered to New Minas Detachment of the RCMP on May 2, 2022.

a. One point of fact that I will highlight is that

the motto on the RCMP's badge translates to "maintain or uphold the right" and that only God – as opposed to Satan, i.e., the god of this world – has the authority to determine what is right. I therefore was being reasonable when I expected the RCMP to get a warrant to arrest the accused that I had named in my cover letter.

i. The general idea that I had was that the police would arrest the accused and charge them under Canada's *Criminal Code*. But because these people's criminal behaviour can readily be explained by "insanity due to demonic possession", these people would be treated for demonic possession instead of being sent to jail.

b. A second point of fact that I will highlight is that I forgot to accuse Queen Elizabeth II (April 21, 1926 – September 8, 2022). Because the Queen is now deceased, we will need to substitute King Charles in her place in order for justice to be served.

9) TAB 5 contains the body of a psychological assessment of Constable Bellingham (RCMP, New Minas Detachment) that is dated May 4, 2022.

10) TAB 6 contains a copy of a letter that I sent to the Kentville Crown Attorney's Office by registered mail that is dated June 3, 2022.

a. In retrospect, I should have explained that the psychological treatment that I had developed for "insanity due to demonic possession" was a spiritual version of electro-convulsive therapy

(ECT) that I had developed and that it could be viewed as akin to an exorcism.

b. I also emailed a copy of this letter to both counsel for Weston Christian Fellowship and Elder Elson, and to Elder Elson, with the subject heading "Good News for Church (Rejoice)". Much to my surprise, neither counsel (Ms. Christina Lazier) nor Elder Elson expressed joy over this letter or even talked to me about this letter. I was disappointed at the time because I had thought that I had not only given the church a gift that it could use in its court case, but that I had also come up with a brilliant idea for how our church could rejuvenate itself for the second coming of Christ.[15]

11) On June 26, 2022, I discovered a copy of Weston Christian Fellowship's "Notice of Intention to Raise Constitutional Argument" – that is dated June 24, 2022 – at an empty table in the church's fellowship room and was shocked by what I had read.

15 When had my IQ tested back in the 1990s, I was told my IQ that was higher than normal. One point of fact that I will mention is that the combination of IQ and Openness (a personality trait) is the best predictor of creativity. Another point of fact that I will raise is that creativity is a component of being a genius and this fact in turn explains why everything that I am explaining seems rather – "elementary" (I am quoting from the movies about Sherlock Holmes). All of this being said, I highlight that these characteristics that I have are gifts from God instead of being anything of my own making and that I am using these gifts to serve God's glory.

12) In early July 2022, I was evicted from Weston Christian Fellowship for speaking truth.

13) TAB 7 contains a copy of a comment that I had posted on Weston Christian Fellowship's Facebook page on July 10, 2022, in which I questioned Ms. Lazier's competence. Because I had anticipated that my comment would be deleted, I also emailed my comment to various members of the congregation so that I would have a time- and date-stamped record of my post.

14) TAB 8 contains a copy of a letter that was addressed to the Kentville Justice Centre and was dated July 25, 2022. In this letter, I again expressed my concerns about Ms. Lazier's incompetence. As one example to demonstrate that Ms. Lazier was not serving the church's or God's interests, I will point out that on page 9 of her "Notice of Intention to Raise Constitutional Argument" she cited *Law Society of British Columbia v. Trinity Western University* as if the Supreme Court of Canada is a credible source of information.

a. An interesting point of fact about King Charles vs. Weston Christian Fellowship and Marty Elson is that all parties (court, counsels, and clients) in this case are in a state of psychosis. This fact in turn explains why I need to intervene in this matter. To state the obvious, everyone involved with the Crown's case against Weston Christian Fellowship and Elder Elson needs the same treatment as everyone involved in the Crown's case against Ms. Guptill and Mr. MacKenzie.

15) On December 6, 2022, I emailed Corporal Tremblay (RCMP) regarding the arrests of Ms. Guptill and Mr. MacKenzie. Much to my surprise, he responded to my email message; but as I should have expected, his response was a non-answer (akin to how Canadian politicians conduct themselves in places such as our legislatures and in Parliament when they are in session). Below is a screenshot of the portion of his message that I thought was particularly interesting:

Cpl. / Cap. Guillaume Tremblay

Public Information Officer, Strategic Communications, Halifax District RCMP
Royal Canadian Mounted Police – Government of Canada
rcmpns-grcne@rcmp-grc.gc.ca

16) On December 7, 2022, I emailed Corporal Tremblay to ask him why was there a dash between the words "Police" and "Government" in his signature [TAB 9]. To state the obvious, the two institutions need to be independent of one another for the purposes of oversight and transparency – two of the hallmarks of a free society. When I did not receive a response from Corporal Tremblay, I thought to myself "Gotcha!" and that it was time to reel everyone in. I saw the situation as akin to the section of the Bible in which Jesus Christ tells Peter that he was currently a fisherman, but that if he followed Jesus, he would become a fisher of men for the purpose of saving their souls (Matthew 4:19 and Mark 1:17; KJV).

17) On December 13, 2022, I emailed the Dartmouth Provincial Court with an offer to intervene in

the Crown's case against Ms. Guptill and Mr. MacKenzie [TAB 10]. To err on the side of caution, I also sent a copy of this email message to the court by registered mail. I later decided to consolidate this case with that of the Crown's case against Weston Christian Fellowship and Elder Elson, and to then write this document in which I am adopting a "grab the bull by his horns" approach instead of a diplomatic approach.

Next Steps

Now that I have outlined the relevant facts, the next step for me is to outline a procedure that integrates all of the relevant facts so that the court can make correct decisions that will benefit all Canadians.

1) The court will need to set up two Case Management Conferences, the first of which should be held in January 2023. Given that it is highly unlikely that all of the other parties will fit at a single desk in a courtroom, I recommend that the court hold the Case Management Conferences on Zoom.

2) At the first Case Management Conference, which will require a half-day, the parties will agree to a procedure by which we can compile all of the names of the people who are in need of an exorcism.[16] As an example to demonstrate the

16 Although the procedure that I have developed to save souls can be viewed as an exorcism or the spiritual equivalent of ECT, I am making reference only to the exorcism so that this section of this document does not become overly wordy.

complexity of this task, I note that once a Crown Attorney has received an exorcism then that person will be in a position to understand the brief that I hand-delivered to the RCMP on May 2, 2022, and to then ensure that all of the people that I accused can be brought to justice.

3) At the second Case Management Conference, which will require a full day, the parties will discuss the particulars of the wording of the court order(s) and a procedure on how to implement it or them. This will likely be a complex task and we may need to invoke the *Emergency Measures Act* and/or shut down this country for 2 weeks if it indeed is the case that all of the following groups of people will be among the ones who will be needing a court-ordered exorcism:

- the entire judiciary and all of the prothonotaries in Canada's courts
- all of the lawyers in Canada (broadly defined to include people such as Ezra Levant, who I understand has a law degree)
- the vast majority of Canada's police officers
- all of Canada's elected officials (past and present), as well as the unelected bureaucrats and public service employees who did their bidding e.g., by staying silent during the "pandemic"
- the vast majority of Canada's health care workers (broadly defined to include workers in both government-funded and private practices) because they of all people should have known better
- the vast majority of Canada's educators (broadly defined to include professors,

teachers, and administrators in Canada's education system)

- all of the people who are in positions of leadership or power within Canada's financial sector
- the entire media industry (broadly defined to include both the mainstream and alternative media who serve corporate interests; citizen journalists such as The Amazing Polly and Dan Dicks of Press for Truth – who to my knowledge are not funded by corporations – would be exempt from the court order given the stellar work that they have done in exposing corruption prior to and during the "pandemic")
- the vast majority if not all of the churches in Nova Scotia
    - In the case of the churches, the court will need to issue an order that explains to them that "The time is fulfilled, and the kingdom of God is at hand; repent ye, and believe the Gospel" (Mark 1:15; KJV) and that what they should be doing is "[preparing] ye the way of the Lord, make his paths straight" (Luke 3:4; KJV).

When the court issues the order(s), it would be a good idea if the presiding Justice started that court session by saying that anyone who actually believed – and in particular if they still believe – that putting underwear on their faces is going protect anyone from the world's deadliest disease is badly in need of a spanking on their bottoms, and that this fact also applies to the people who thought that it was a good idea to get injected with an experimental drug without informed consent. And lest the people who did not drink the COVID Kool-Aid have a false sense of moral superiority over those who did, the Justice will need to remind Canadians that many of these people are also in or at risk for being in a state of psychosis. I note that many of the people who did not drink the COVID Kool-Aid follow a New Age philosophy that talks about a universal god or consciousness, and includes strange advice to people such as hugging "heart-to-heart" and "keeping their vibrations up". From a Biblical perspective, these people are making the mistake of worshipping God's creations instead of God and therefore are being deceived by Satan; the easiest way to remedy this problem is by them using their free will to turn to the true God who is committed to serving humanity's interests.

My professional opinion is that the Bible is the perfect work of art because it comforts the afflicted and afflicts the comfortable by telling them that which they do not want to hear. The fact that people who are comfortable do not like to be afflicted explains what Jesus Christ meant when He explained that the world hates Him because the world hates the one that sent Him, i.e., our Father and Creator who tells us "thou shalt not..." instead of "do what thou wilt". Unfortunately, most Christians do not realize that they are trying to serve two masters or are worshipping a non-existent version of Jesus Christ, and that this approach is leading them to the fires of hell.

4) Because Canada's legal system has Satanic origins, the easiest way to exorcise them is by no longer relying on Black's Law Dictionary as the foundation of this country's legal system given

that we already have the Bible. A court order to Dalhousie University's Law School to remove this book from its curriculum would be a good start.

Closing Comments

A point of fact about Donald Trump's tenure as President of the United States of America is that he did not keep his election promise to Make America Great Again (MAGA) by draining the swamp. For example, he abandoned his election promise to have Hilary Clinton put in jail. If my understanding is correct, this happened because MAGA is not only a campaign slogan, but is also the fifth and highest degree in the Church of Satan's hierarchy. If true, then this would readily explain why Donald Trump did not keep his election promise. The good news here, though, is that I am relying on Christ and Biblical principles (e.g., "spare the rod, spoil the child [of God]") to Make Canada Great Again (MCGA), and on Christ to drain the swamp given that it is clear that – in the same way that budgets do not balance themselves – swamps do not drain themselves.

I look forward to working with everyone!

Blessings,

Rakesh ("Rick") Mehta, PhD
Cognitive Psychologist & Defender of Truth

Email: rick.mehta@hotmail.com
Phone: (902) 678-5876

CC: Provincial Court (Kentville)
Crown Attorney's Office, Dartmouth
Crown Attorney's Office, Kentville
Ms. Christina Lazier, Counsel for Weston Christian Fellowship and Marty Elson
Elder Marty Elson
Ms. Morgan May Guptill (via email; she can forward this message to Mr. Jeremy MacKenzie)

Index of Supporting Documents[17]

TAB 1 Mehta, R., Body of Affidavit 1 (KEN No. 506242; Sworn to on July 8, 2021)

TAB 2 Mehta, R., Body of Affidavit 2 (KEN No. 506242; Sworn to on November 30, 2021)

TAB 3 Mehta, R., Body of Letter that was mailed to Kentville Crown Attorney's Office (March 8, 2022)

TAB 4 Mehta, R., Cover Letter of Brief that was Hand-Delivered to New Minas Detachment of RCMP (May 2, 2022)

TAB 5 Mehta, R., Body of Letter that was sent to Constable Bellingham, New Minas Detachment of RCMP (May 4, 2022)

TAB 6 Mehta, R., Cover Letter of Correspondence that was sent to Kentville Crown Attorney's Office by Registered Mail (June 3, 2022)

TAB 7 Mehta, R., Email message to members of Weston Christian Fellowship's congregation (July 10, 2022)

TAB 8 Mehta, R., Letter that was mailed to Kentville Justice Centre (July 25, 2022)

17 These documents are in Section 2 of this book.

TAB 9 Mehta, R., Email message to Corporal G. Tremblay, RCMP (December 7, 2022)

TAB 10 Mehta, R. Email message to Dartmouth Provincial Court (December 13, 2022)

SECTION 2

TAB 1: BODY OF AFFIDAVIT 1
(July 8, 2021)

2021 Ken No. 506242

Supreme Court of Nova Scotia

Between:

Rakesh ("Rick") Mehta Plaintiff

and

Wolfville Animal Hospital
Dr. Carrie Terry Family
Dentistry Inc. Defendants

Affidavit of Rakesh ("Rick") Mehta

I make oath and give evidence as follows:

1 I am Rakesh ("Rick") Mehta, a whistleblower, an expert witness on the understanding of human nature, a defender of truth, and the mover of the Notice of Motion. Since I am not allowed to call myself a "psychologist" in Nova Scotia due to regulations stipulated by the Nova Scotia Board of Examiners in Psychology, I refer to myself as a behavioural scientist. I am under the

impression that I am pursuing this matter without legal representation because it is a political "hot potato" that no lawyer in Nova Scotia wants to touch, which has undermined my right to legal representation in this proceeding. I am also under the impression that the legal profession in Nova Scotia has been "policing" which cases are heard in our courts, which speaks to concerns I have regarding "abuse of process" and "obstruction of justice".

2 I have personal knowledge of the evidence sworn to in this affidavit except where otherwise stated to be based on information and belief.

3 In this affidavit, I state the source of any information that is not based on my own personal knowledge and I state my belief of the source. I also state that I submit this affidavit with the understanding that – unlike the conduct that I observed by Justices Gabriel and Warner during my divorce proceeding (Vermeiren v. Mehta, 2019) – the judge in this proceeding will be acting in good faith, i.e., in keeping with the principle of "clean hands" as opposed to engaging in "abuse of process" and in keeping with the principle of truth instead of social justice. I point out to the court that, while it is true that Jesus Christ came to save rather than to condemn ("For God sent not his Son into the world to condemn the world; but that the world through him might be saved.", John 3:17, King James Version), he also did tell us that all of us would be judged by our own words ("For by thy words thou shalt be justified, and by thy words thou shalt be condemned", Matthew 12:37, King James Version). For this reason, I strongly encourage the judge to

choose his or her words wisely in their decision.

4

1) The first section of this affidavit speaks to my academic credentials.

2) "**TAB 1**" contains a copy of a letter that I wrote to Dr. Peter Ricketts (President, Acadia University) on January 12, 2019, in which I made my case for promotion to Full Professor. I sent this letter because I was attempting to force my opponents (Acadia University and the Acadia University Faculty Association) to settle the employment dispute that I had with them after my employment as a tenured professor was terminated without cause.

3) "**TAB 2**" contains a copy of the academic resume that I had sent to Dr. Ricketts. The section on my teaching does not include all of my accomplishments (e.g., the fact that enrollment in the courses that cover the biological bases of behavior increased after I started teaching those courses) and does not contain a description of all of the pedagogical techniques that I used in my classes.

4) As a point of fact, my average course instructor rating across my entire career (averaging across both required courses and courses taken as electives) is 4.43 on a scale of 1 to 5, with 4 being "good" and 5 being "very good". That being said, there were four occasions when my average instructor rating was below 4.0; there were extenuating

circumstances at play in my personal life on each of these occasions that impaired my teaching (e.g., my mum had a stroke in the winter semester of the 2012-2013 academic year). My average course rating across my entire career was 4.12.

5) I note that my service record is extensive, which speaks to my ability to work well with others.

6) To the letter that I sent to Dr. Ricketts on January 12, 2019, I attached a copy of the last research presentation that I did while I was employed as a tenured professor at Acadia University. "**TAB 3**" contains a copy of this presentation, which was titled "The Relationship Between Political Orientation and Bullshit Detection in Canadian Politics: Results from a Pilot Study". In case the court has the impression that I am a provocateur because of the title of the presentation, I assure the court that "bullshit detection" is a topic that is being researched within psychology and that there were two other presentations on this topic at the Canadian Society for Brain, Behaviour and Cognitive Science conference where I had made this presentation in July 2018 (The titles of those presentations were: "Bullshit Makes the Art Grow Profounder: Evidence for False Meaning Transfer Across Domains" and "Finding Meaning in the Clouds: Illusory Pattern Perception Predicts Bullshit Receptivity"). With regard to relevance, the take-home message for the court is that a)

leftists/progressives were the least likely to detect that an obviously false statement was bullshit (in part because they do not have a moral compass; see also Dennis Prager's and Prager University's videos that cover the topic of how leftists think and reason about the world around them in comparison to the way people who are not indoctrinated with leftist ideology think and reason about the world around them), b) that these individuals are overrepresented in Nova Scotia's legal profession and judiciary, and c) that this overrepresentation is a barrier to justice.

7) In the letter that I sent to Dr. Ricketts, I made reference to the "Grievance Hoax Studies" that had recently been published and was a topic of much discussion and debate. "**TAB 4**" contains a copy of the text from this publication in which the researchers submitted fake studies to top academic journals and managed to get the studies published – often with glowing reviews – in part because the fake studies told the reviewers and editors what they wanted to hear.

8) Of the studies in this research, the one that is most directly relevant to this proceeding given my earlier reference to feminism being a cancer to society is the study in which the researchers took a chapter from Hitler's "Mein Kampf", substituted feminist jargon in place of anti-Semitic jargon, and were successful in getting the study published.

9) In my capacity as an expert witness, I strongly recommend that decision makers in the legal system also read the works and/or watch the videos (where relevant) of free thinkers such as Janice Fiamengo (former professor of English at the University of Ottawa and longtime Canadian critic of feminism; host of the Fiamengo File on YouTube), David Solway, and Philip Carl Salzman, and read works that have been published by other free thinkers in forums such as Quillette, Aero, or Spiked magazines. In the same way that a carpenter can do only so much if all that person has to work with is a hammer or saw, justice cannot be administered or served unless the courts are aware of the various ways in which the problems that they have been tasked to solve can be conceptualized and analyzed.

10) Since the Grievance Hoax Studies was published, two of the three authors (Helen Pluckrose and James Lindsay) went on to publish the following book for the general public: "Cynical Theories: How Activist Scholarship Made Everything about Race, Gender, and Identity – And Why This Harms Everybody".

11) Another book that was recently published that is relevant to decision making in a court of law is one published by Gad Saad that is titled "The Parasitic Mind: How Infectious Ideas are Killing Common Sense". If the court has the impression that I am recommending Dr. Saad's book because he interviewed me

on two episodes of the Saad Truth (the title of Dr. Saad's YouTube channel), "**TAB 5**" demonstrates that Dr. Saad has blocked me on Twitter. My understanding is that for reasons that are unclear to me, he now refers to me as an "asshole".

12) This list of sources that I have referenced in this proceeding is far from comprehensive.

13) The second section of this affidavit speaks to my uncovering of widespread corruption in the legislation that has been enacted by federal, provincial, and municipal governments, e.g., I made reference to Code of Conduct that is signed by all municipal councilors in Nova Scotia and to the past sexual misconduct of the Deputy Mayor of the Town of Wolfville (Oonagh Proudfoot) in the documents that counsels for the defendants received when they were served.

14) "**TAB 6**" contains a copy of the campaign brochure that I circulated in the 2020 municipal election, which speaks to my character and values.

15) Since counsel for Dr. Terry's clinic had accused me of engaging in "abuse of process" in his client's Notice of Defence, "**TAB 7**" contains a copy of an email message that I sent to Kentville Town Council on June 29, 2021, in which I pointed out that – in the words of counsel for the Wolfville Animal Hospital – "with greater freedom and autonomy to conduct their own affairs,

without oversight by a provincial or federal government" comes an opportunity for the municipal governments in Nova Scotia to engage in "abuse of process".

16) The email message described in the previous paragraph was sent to not only the members of Kentville Town Council, but also to a) Geoff Muttart because he was the solicitor at the meeting of council that was held on May 30, 2021, and b) counsel for the Municipality of the County of Kings (the mayor is Peter Muttart, who also happens to be Geoff's father) because I live in Coldbook instead of Kentville. I hope that – especially after reading the next paragraph – the court will agree with my assessment that the word "shit-show" is an accurate term for describing the current state of Canadian politics and Canada's legal system.

17) Since counsel for Dr. Terry's clinic is interested in "abuse of process", I will summarize key examples (i.e., a bird's eye perspective) of this principle in Canada's recent history. In the 1960s, the civil rights movement that was started by people such as Martin Luther King, Jr., was hijacked by Marxists and marked the first wave of the politicization of our universities. In 1981, Prime Minster Pierre Elliott Trudeau implemented the Canadian Charter of Rights and Freedoms into law, with help from Queen Elizabeth II, and started the process of governments stacking our courts with political activists. Let us not forget that a hallmark of

PET's tenure was dividing Canadians against each other along regional and linguistic lines, e.g., his reference to "regional loyalties" in his signatory statement on the Charter.

In 1989 (the same year that the Berlin Wall fell, which marked the start of the second wave of the politicization of our universities, e.g., nonsensical notions such as "implicit bias", "stereotype threat", and "microaggressions" started to be incorporated into university curricula; around this time, universities started to take feminists and postmodernism more seriously), the Nova Scotia government implemented the Nova Scotia Trade Union Act and Nova Scotia Human Rights Act into law, both of which set the stage for unions and clown/kangaroo courts to have – to borrow wording from counsel for the Wolfville Animal Hospital – "freedom and autonomy to conduct their own affairs without oversight". For unions, a major victory was reached in Weber v. Ontario Hydro (1995) because this Supreme Court of Canada ruling gave unions full carriage rights on their members' cases but without any requirement for the unions to be accountable to their members; however, this decision would not have been possible without decisions starting in 1984 to set the stage for the 1995 ruling.

According to the web site of Nathanson Seaman Watts, it was only "in the last 20 years" that the Municipal Government Act (1998; amended 2000) was implemented, which gave our municipalities not only an opportunity to demonstrate responsible stewardship ("With such autonomy comes increased responsibility"), but also an opportunity to engage in "abuse of process". Because I have been presented with no evidence to demonstrate to me that Mr. Nathanson or Mr. Cuming act in good faith (e.g., the web site for Nathanson Seaman Watts states that the lawyers at this firm "look for ways to resolve a dispute in a fair and reasonable manner before it gets to court" but Mr. Nathanson never responded to any of correspondence that I sent him with the hope that reaching out to him would prevent me from having to go to court), the only reasonable conclusion that I can derive is that they and the other lawyers with whom they have a "casual connection" interpreted the implementation of the Municipal Government Act as an opportunity to participate in "a specialized area of law that requires experience and expertise" in "abuse of process".

The year 2015 ("Because it's 2015.") marked the third wave of the politicization of our universities and the further breakdown of Canada's social fabric as Prime Minster Justin Trudeau spent the first part of his tenure dividing Canadians along every line possible (in the Bible, Jesus Christ makes reference to a house divided being easy to conquer, i.e., "And Jesus…said unto them, Every kingdom divided against itself is brought to desolation, and every city or house divided against itself shall not stand", Matthew 12:25, King James Version) and capitalizing on political movements such as Me Too for personal and political gain, while turning a blind eye to his own misconduct and the misconduct of individuals associated with him and the Pierre Elliott Trudeau Foundation; this preceded Event 201 and the unleashing of the Wuhan virus (as documented in Archbishop Viganò's open letter to POTUS Trump).

18) In summary, Mr. Cuming is correct when he brings up the notion of "abuse of process". However, the spirit in which he brings up this notion seems entirely consistent with quotations attributed to Joseph Goebbels (Minister of Propaganda for Germany's Nazi Party) and seems to apply directly and entirely to the defendants and their counsels: a) "Accuse the other side of that which you are guilty", b) "Keep the lie big, keep it simple, keep saying it and eventually they will believe it", c) "If you repeat a lie often enough, people will believe it and you will come to believe it yourself".

19) The third (and final) section of this affidavit speaks to Satan being the mastermind behind COVID-19 and links the following parties with Satan: Prime Minster Justin Trudeau, Dr. Peter Ricketts (President, Acadia University, and Ms. Erin Patterson (Past President, Acadia University Faculty Association).

20) A point of fact is that people in free societies have the choice of swearing on the Bible or a

book of laws before giving testimony in their courts of law. My understanding is that the book of laws was used in these courtrooms so that people who are not Christians would not be required to swear on a book that went against their beliefs in order to have their testimony accepted as valid in a court of law. If my understanding is correct, the validity of the book of laws can be measured by assessing how closely it stays true to principles that are in the Bible or, worded somewhat differently, the extent to which the laws that mere humans have derived are true to the word and spirit of God's law.

21) The legal definition of "defamation" refers to the dissemination of false statements about a person to third parties. This definition is similar to the commandment in the Bible that tells us "Thou shalt not bear false witness against thy neighbor" (Exodus 20:16, King James Version).

22) One of the defences to defamation is justification (truth). This begs the question of what is truth? According to the Bible, Jesus Christ is the definition of not only truth, but also life, i.e., "I am the way, the truth, and the life" (John 14:6; King James Version).

23) A fact that I raised in Ken. No. 506256 (Mehta v. Acadia University and Acadia University Faculty Association) is that the word "lie" is interchangeable with the term "social justice". Related to this issue, the

acronym for the components of social justice (Diversity, Inclusion, and Equity) is DIE.

24) If Jesus Christ represents truth and life, whereas the goal of social justice is death, then it stands to reason that Satan is the mastermind behind social justice because social justice is based on lies, i.e., Jesus Christ = truth and life; Satan = lies (social justice) and death.

25) As I had explained in Ken. No. 506256, I first became concerned about the issue of ideological conformity within our universities and their implications for free speech when Dr. Ricketts stated that he planned to commit Acadia University to social justice. I have included a copy of the letter that I submitted to the Presidential Search Committee on March 27, 2017, in "**TAB 8**".

26) "**TAB 9**" contains the letter that I sent to Acadia University on December 17, 2019, in which I informed the university that I planned to take the institution to court for defamation.

27) "**TAB 10**" contains the response that Acadia University sent me on December 20, 2019, in which a Vice President (Chris Callbeck) thanked me for my letter. I include this correspondence because I am under the impression that the university was happy about the upcoming litigation, which seems rather odd to me.

28) On February 9, 2020, I met with "Father" John MacPherson and Mr. Phil Kenny at Mr. MacPherson's office in St. Joseph's Catholic Church (also known as Corpus Christi Parish) in Kentville, Nova Scotia. During that meeting, I was made to feel unwelcome in the church community because I was a former professor at Acadia University (no reference was made to my conduct in the church community during this meeting), which made me decide to leave the church. Shortly after the meeting, I noticed that the most recent section of the course that I was taking at the church in order to be baptized into the Roman Catholic faith was titled the Catechumenate section. The photos in "**TAB 11**" show that the 16th Catechumenate calls on Christians to "establish social justice". Interestingly, the supporting text from the Bible makes reference only to "justice", not "social justice", which tells us that the text in the Catechumenate is based on a lie and supports Archbishop Viganò's claim regarding the presence of a deep church in society. Even more interesting (in a morbidly fascinating sense) is that the short form for the 16th Catechumenate is C16, i.e., the bill that Dr. Jordan B. Peterson (University of Toronto) spoke out against because of its implications for suppressing free speech. Anyone following cases such as those of Jessica Yaniv or the child custody case that is taking place in BC involving a child who likely is suffering from rapid onset gender dysphoria can tell you that Bill C-16 had implications that were more far-reaching than what Dr. Peterson and Dr.

Saad testified to in their appearances before the Canadian Senate.

29) On March 3, 2020, Prime Minister Justin Trudeau made a "surprise appearance" at a citizenship ceremony held at Acadia University in the Town of Wolfville. Dr. Ricketts appeared on the same stage as the Prime Minister during the ceremony. On the same day, Prime Minister Justin Trudeau visited the Noodle Guy, a restaurant co-owned by Ms. Erin Patterson (Past President of the Acadia University Faculty Association on the day in question; she was also chief negotiator of the Fifteenth Collective Agreement Between the Board and Acadia University Faculty Association, which is the guise under which Acadia University had terminated my employment as a tenured professor without cause; she is currently a political candidate for the Nova Scotia New Democratic Party). "**TAB 12**" contains photos of Dr. Ricketts and Ms. Patterson with Prime Minister Trudeau that were taken on March 3, 2020. A fact I wish to highlight is that Ms. Patterson made the following comment on Facebook: "Quite an exciting day at the Noodle Guy! Our MP Kodi Blois brought his boss to lunch." I thought that the comment was interesting because my campaign brochure made reference to me "serving" the interests of my constituents; I did not state the following point in my campaign brochure, but if anyone had asked me who is my "boss", I would have responded "Jesus Christ".

30) As a point of fact, the Prime Minister's visit took place one day prior to him announcing the creation of a Cabinet Committee by the federal government, supposedly to "limit the spread of the virus" and to protect the "health and safety of all Canadians" (according to what I had read on Wikipedia in March 2021).

31) An interesting and unusual point of fact regarding policies in response to COVID-19 is that there is uniform or "lockstep" agreement between the federal government and both their provincial and municipal counterparts, as well as compliance from the vast majority (if not all) of the churches in Nova Scotia, e.g., apart from the issue that there is an apparent absence of our churches ministering to the sick and dying during this "pandemic", I am unaware of an Atlantic counterpart to Pastor Coates, Pastor Hildebrandt, or Pastor Pawlowski. In "TAB 24" of the Affidavit of Documents that counsels for the defendants received when they were served, I wrote: "And according to historians such as Pierre Burton, Canada's glory days ended with the Diefenbaker era. Based on this and the fact that Stephen Harper once referred to Atlantic Canada as a "culture of defeat" and that Ralph Klein once referred to Atlantic Canadians as "Eastern bastards who deserve to freeze in the dark" – and that to my knowledge these statements have never been proven false – I strongly suspect that the deep state took hold in this time frame and started in Atlantic Canada." A

famous moment during Premier Klein's career occurred in 1990 when – in his capacity as environment minister – he gave a one-finger salute to environmental activists. A response such as this one from the Supreme Court of Nova Scotia to the people and the forces of darkness who wish to enslave humanity would demonstrate to the public and to Jesus Christ that the court believes that "every child [of God] matters".

Sworn to before me)
on ____________________, 2021)
at Kentville, NS.)

____

Rakesh ("Rick") Mehta

Index of Supporting Documents[18]

Mehta v. Wolfville Animal Hospital & Dr. Carrie Terry
Family Dentistry Inc. (2021)
Ken No. 506242

TAB 1 Letter from R. Mehta to Dr. Peter Ricketts (President and Vice-Chancellor, Acadia University) (January 12, 2019).

TAB 2 R. Mehta. Academic Resume.

TAB 3 Copy of R. Mehta's Poster Presentation at the 28th Annual Meeting of the Canadian Society for Brain, Behaviour and Cognitive Science (July 2018). "The Relationship Between Political Orientation and Bullshit Detection in Canadian Politics: Results from a Pilot Study".

TAB 4 Text of research published in Aero Magazine: Lindsay, J.A., Boghossian, P., and Pluckrose, H. (2018). Academic Grievance Studies and the Corruption of Scholarship.

TAB 5 Screenshot from R. Mehta's Twitter account to demonstrate that Gad Saad has blocked him on Twitter

TAB 6 R. Mehta. Campaign brochure for 2020 municipal election.

18 These documents were included with the affidavit that I swore to at the courthouse in Kentville, Nova Scotia, but are not being included in this book.

TAB 7 Email message from R. Mehta to Kentville Town Council (June 29, 2021)

TAB 8 Letter from R. Mehta to Acadia University's Presidential Search Committee (March 27, 2017)

TAB 9 Letter from R. Mehta to Mr. Chris Callbeck (Vice President Finance & Administration and CFO, Acadia University). (December 17, 2019).

Attached to letter:

1) Letter to Dr. Morrison, Vice President Advancement (November 15, 2019)
2) Email Message to Dr. Rod Morrison, Vice President Advancement (May 5, 2019)

TAB 10 Letter from Mr. Chris Callbeck (Vice President Finance & Administration and CFO, Acadia Univeristy) to R. Mehta (20 December 2019)

TAB 11 Photographs of Catechumenate 16 (Material in RCIA course at St. Joseph's Catholic Church)

TAB 12 Photographs from Prime Minister Justin Trudeau's visit to Acadia University (March 3, 2020)

TAB 2: BODY OF AFFIDAVIT 2
(November 30, 2021)

2021	Ken No. 506242

Supreme Court of Nova Scotia

Between:

Rakesh ("Rick") Mehta	Plaintiff
and	
Wolfville Animal Hospital Dr. Carrie Terry Family Dentistry Inc.	Defendants

Affidavit of Rakesh ("Rick") Mehta

I make oath and give evidence as follows:

1 I am Dr. Rakesh ("Rick") Mehta, a natural person who – by virtue of being born in the land of Canada – has inalienable God-given rights that are enshrined in the laws of this land that can be traced to historic documents such as the King James Version of the Bible and the Magna Carta; in contrast, the health care clinics are corporations that are governed by rules enshrined in admiralty

law. Had the court's web site made it clear that I could pursue this matter under common law procedures, I would have done so. But because the court's web site makes reference only to Rules of Civil Procedure, I am pursuing this matter under admiralty law. I expect the court to not penalize me for its negligence.

2 I am submitting this affidavit in response to the defendants' Notice of Motion to dismiss my case (the court session is scheduled for December 14, 2021). In my affidavit dated July 8, 2021, I noted that I was pursuing this matter without legal representation because I was under the impression that the legal profession in Nova Scotia has been "policing" which cases are heard in our courts, which speaks to concerns I had regarding "abuse of process" and "obstruction of justice" on the part of the legal profession. More recently, I have learned that it is a fact that the Government of Nova Scotia has retained the services of all of the law firms in this province and that this fact explains why I was unable to retain counsel for this proceeding. Given that the counsels did not disclose this fact, I will not be paying their legal fees and will instead direct them to send their bills to the Government of Nova Scotia given that the counsels are serving the government's interests instead of their clients' interests; an unintended consequence of the counsels' actions is that they have placed themselves in a position of conflict of interest in which they have been unable to give their clients (the health care

clinics) sound legal advice. In Section 3 of this affidavit, I will explain to the counsels and the court the consequences of the counsels' actions because they have had – in the words of counsel for the Wolfville Animal Hospital – "real implications for real people".

2 I have personal knowledge of the evidence sworn to in this affidavit except where otherwise stated to be based on information and belief.

3 In this affidavit, I state the source of any information that is not based on my own personal knowledge and I state my belief of the source. I also state that Mr. Timothy D. Hergett (Hergett Law Inc.) advised me that a lawyer who has a strong case will argue on the basis of facts whereas a lawyer who has a weak case or no case will argue on the basis of posturing and doublespeak (known colloquially as "talking out of one's ass"). At the court session that was held on October 29, 2021 (the court did not inform me that the session was a "case management conference"), I was perplexed by the fact that Justice Arnold and the counsels were discussing the Rules instead of the facts of this case given that I already knew for a fact that the prothonotary's job is to obstruct justice by coming up with excuses to refuse to accept documents by self-represented litigants because they do not meet the arbitrary and nonsensical criteria specified in the Rules. Worded somewhat differently, given that the prothonotary had processed my Notice of Motion, it is a fact that Justice Arnold and counsels were being disingenuous during the court session that was held on October 29 and that the counsels are lying in their Notice of Motion given that they had originally supported my Notice of Motion

– which is the only reason why the prothonotary had processed my motion in the first place. If the court and counsels object to me pointing out these facts to them, I remind them that my last research presentation was on the topic of bullshit detection in Canadian politics, which they can verify for themselves by reviewing the affidavit that I submitted in July. In summary, the fact of this matter is that the barrier to justice has little to nothing to do with me or my conduct, but the fact that the counsels, prothonotaries, and judiciary at the Supreme Court of Nova Scotia are not only tyrants who revel in their power, but are also people who exhibit the Dunning-Kruger effect – which Dr. Gad Saad characterizes as "a self-assuredness and supreme confidence despite one's idiocy" (page 13) in his book "The Parasitic Mind: How Infectious Ideas are Killing Common Sense", e.g., the court attempting to pressure me into signing the "Undertaking And Agreement of Non-Lawyer Form" that contains a field titled "Name of Lawyer, if any".

4

1) My affidavit dated July 8, 2021, spoke to my academic credentials, the widespread corruption in our societal and democratic institutions, and the fact that Satan is the mastermind behind COVID-19; worded somewhat differently, that affidavit proved that Dr. Strang and other high-ranking officials have ties to Satan, i.e., they are under Satan's influence and/or are taking direction from Satan. This affidavit speaks to the fact that the counsels, their clients, and the court have been derelict in their duties.

2) I chose to take these health care clinics to

court because, unlike other corporations, the owners of these clinics have sworn an oath and/or have an ethical obligation to serve the public's interests. "**TAB 1**" contains a screenshot of the Canadian Veterinary Oath and "**TAB 2**" contains a copy of the Provincial Dental Board of Nova Scotia's Code of Ethics. To state the obvious, these health care clinics have a duty to look out for the interests of the public and their clients instead of the interests of the government. Given the obvious negligence on their part, my understanding is that I am in a position to sue for financial compensation but instead have chosen to use our courts to have the Health Protection Act order overturned as unconstitutional because it is a fact that the order is a clear case of abuse of power.

3) To transition to the issues of what the owners of the health care clinics ought to have known and what legal advice the counsels should have given their clients, I will reiterate that I became a Christian in February 2019 and that I was evicted from the Catholic church in February 2020. Shortly after my eviction, I noticed that the church's course materials made reference to Bill C-16 (the bill that Dr. Jordan B. Peterson had opposed) and the fact that the 16th Catechumenate called Christians to the cause of social justice, whereas the Bible makes reference only to justice, i.e., the information in the 16th Catechumenate is a lie. As well, I noticed that Prime Minister Justin Trudeau visited Acadia University one day prior to him announcing the creation of a Cabinet Committee by the federal government, supposedly to "limit the spread

of the virus" and to protect the "health and safety of all Canadians" (according to what I had read on Wikipedia in March 2021).

4) Related to the previous paragraph, a point of fact worth highlighting is that COVID-19 appeared on the world stage in the year 2020, which can also be depicted as 20/20, i.e., perfect acuity or the year that all would start to become clear in the sense of being revealed (i.e., Book of Revelation). Another point of fact that is worth highlighting is that the Book of Revelation states that "…for by thy sorceries were all nations deceived." (Revelation, 18:23; KJV). The Greek translation for "sorceries" is pharmakeia (pharmaceuticals). When combined with the facts that a) in the Cold War, President Ronald Reagan said that the battle of our time was moral and spiritual, and that Prime Minister Pierre Elliott Trudeau did not include the references to morality and spirituality in the Charter that were included in the Canadian Bill of Rights, and b) the acronym for the components of social justice (Diversity, Inclusion, and Equity) is DIE because social justice is based on lies (in contrast to Jesus Christ representing truth and life), an important fact in this matter is that we are living in the midst of the closing stages of a war that is taking place between God and Satan in the spiritual realm that is manifesting itself in our physical world.

5) In April 2020, Dr. Denis Rancourt (Researcher, Ontario Civil Liberties Association) published an article that was

widely disseminated that is titled "Masks Don't Work: A Review of Science Relevant to COVID-19 Social Policy" ("**TAB 3**"). Had the owners of the clinics exercised due diligence instead of accepting the recommendations of Drs. Strang and Tam at face value, they would have known early on during the "pandemic" that public health officials were not serving the public's interests.

6) "**TAB 4**" contains a copy of an article that Mr. John Carpay (President, Justice Centre for Constitutional Freedoms) published on July 25, 2020, in which he explains how mandatory mask policies have no basis in science or law. Had the counsels not been in a conflict of interest position, they could have advised their clients to not comply with the Health Protection Act order.

7) A fact that I will raise at this stage is that I knew back in July 2020 that the Justice Centre for Constitutional Freedoms and other constitutional lawyers would be unsuccessful in fighting the emergency measures in court (e.g., the recent ruling in Manitoba) because the words "reasonable limits" in the Charter allow for our courts to arbitrarily take away Canadian citizens' rights. This fact explains why my legal arguments in my Notice of Motion speak to the introduction of the Charter rather than the body of the Charter (i.e., before the words "reasonable limits").

8) The Government of Nova Scotia implemented a mandatory mask policy in or around July or August 2020.

9) On October 25, 2020 (in the proximity of the time that I had expressed my concerns to the Wolfville Animal Hospital), Archbishop Carlo Maria Viganò published an open letter to President of the United States (POTUS) Donald J. Trump in which he explained how COVID-19 is part of a "global conspiracy against God and humanity" (**"TAB 5"**). This document is of central importance to this matter because the court and counsels for the defendants are working under the false premise that we are living in the midst of a "pandemic" and that the use of face masks is going to protect people from the world's deadliest disease. To the contrary of the court's and counsels' understanding of world affairs, common sense would dictate that – even if we were in the midst of a pandemic – it is not a good idea for people to breathe the waste products that they are exhaling. At the court sessions that I have attended, I have noticed that I may well have been the only person in the courtroom who wore glasses. If others in the room were paying attention, they would have noticed that my glasses were fogging up. This fogging demonstrates the fact that the face masks are creating a moist environment on people's faces that provides ideal conditions for infectious agents to grow and therefore will not protect people's health. In addition, it is a fact that containers for so-called "medical masks" often include a disclaimer that states that these masks are ineffective against viruses and it is a fact that the lining of the "medical masks" often contains graphene.

10) On October 23, 2020, I submitted a letter to Dr. Natasha Cairns (who runs the Wolfville Animal Hospital) in which I expressed my concerns regarding the clinic's policies in response to COVID-19 ("**TAB 6**"). In this letter, I provided evidence for my concern that the policies that governments have implemented have no basis in science or law, and that the clinic was implementing policies that were more stringent than those implemented by the Government of Nova Scotia. I substantiated my beliefs with mortality data, a tweet by constitutional lawyer Mr. Rocco Galati (Constitutional Rights Centre) demonstrating that rates of sickness are higher in people who wear face masks than those who do not, and referencing three books by Dr. Judi Mikovits (the scientist who blew the whistle on Dr. Anthony Fauci of the World Health Organization). The books by Dr. Mikovits make reference to or imply corruption in science and/or medicine. Based on this collective evidence, I stated to Dr. Cairns that her actions were counterproductive to her goal of "keeping everyone safe".

11) On October 27, 2020, Dr. Cairns sent me a letter in which she dismissed me as a client from the Wolfville Animal Hospital ("**TAB 7**"). Specifically, she started her letter by stating "Unfortunately, the **policy** in place at the Wolfville Animal Hospital regarding the wearing of masks does not conform with your beliefs or expectations" and concluded her letter by stating that "we **must** do the best that we can given the **guidelines** set forth to us from our governing body" (emphases

added to highlight discrepancies). She also cited her blind obedience to policies set by the Nova Scotia Veterinary Medical Association and Nova Scotia Department of Health over her oath as evidence of herself being "honest [and having] very strong moral principles". Contrary to her claim that she has integrity and has morals, it is clear that Dr. Cairns prioritizes "standing by [the] clinic policy as a whole and undivided veterinary team" over the health concerns of the owners of her patients or the fact that there is substantial corruption in the fields of science and/or medicine, which has clear implications for the patients that are under her care.

12) Related to the errors of commission in Dr. Cairns' letter that I described in the previous paragraph, her letter to me also included errors of omission. Her letter to me did not refute the facts or arguments that I had presented in my letter to her; worded somewhat differently, Dr. Cairns did not explain to me how my beliefs were mistaken. As well, her letter did not explain to me how the letter I had submitted to her was written in the spirit of dishonesty or the absence of truth. If anything, because Dr. Cairns was aware of the challenges that I faced when my employment as a tenured professor at Acadia University was terminated for speaking truth, she ought to have known that – while I make no claim to being without sin – I have a solid track record when it comes to the issue of integrity and therefore am a credible source of information.

13) On February 3, 2021, I emailed Dr. Terry's office to inform the clinic that I could no

longer continue to come to her clinic because her clinic was implementing policies that have no basis in science or law ("**TAB 8**"). In this message, I included a copy of a message I had submitted to Dr. Ann Collins (President, Canadian Medical Association; henceforth, CMA) via the CMA's web site on January 30 in which I stated that it was the CMA's own fault that public health authorities are being questioned by members of the public. In his response to me, Dr. Terry's secretary referred to COVID-19 as a "pandemic", claimed that the clinic "has to trust" the government, and implied that everyone's views regarding COVID-19 is of equal value or respect. In my response, I explained to Dr. Terry's clinic the errors in the logic and reasoning behind the response that I had received. I also made reference to a book co-authored by Klaus Schwab of the World Economic Forum that is titled "COVID-19: The Great Reset" that anyone can purchase from web sites such as Amazon or Chapters, and pointed out that this book is a modern day version of books such as Hitler's "Mein Kampf" or Marx's "Communist Manifesto". I also made reference to atrocities committed in World War 2 by people who were merely "following orders". Finally, I suggested that Dr. Terry watch the video on my YouTube channel that is titled "Silencing Dissent" (the full title of the presentation in the video is titled "Safe Space Culture in Canadian Universities: An Assault on our Democracy"), which documents my struggle with Acadia University and the wide-spread corruption in Canada's education system.

14) On April 8, 2021, I emailed Dr. Terry to ask her if she is failing to uphold her oath when she is continuing to implement policies that have no basis in science or law (“**TAB 9**”). I stated that this question was based on the premise that dentists swear to principles akin to those in the Hippocratic Oath, which includes the principle to do no harm. I also asked her if she did not have a duty to dissent for the sake of defending her patients’ interests when it is clear that the policies that are in place have been implemented by a provincial government and a regulatory board that are corrupt.

15) On April 8, 2021, Dr. Terry emailed me to state that she was dismissing me from her clinic. In her response to me, Dr. Terry claimed that she did not know why I “felt” that the current legislation is unlawful and admitted that she runs her clinic based on her feelings instead of an objective review of evidence. Dr. Terry did not provide me with an answer to my question about dentists swearing to principles that are similar to those in the Hippocratic Oath or with an answer to my other question.

16) In the dismissal letter that Dr. Terry attached to her email message to me, Dr. Terry wrote: “Please be advised that due to your current stance on our office policies for reopening (after being shut down by the NS government for COVID-19) we can no longer continue to provide care”.

17) On May 7, 2021, Dr. Terry emailed me to ask me to send future correspondence

regarding this dispute to Mr. Gérald Mallet of Sedgwick Canada Inc. instead of her lawyer (Mr. Cuming), which I did later that day ("**TAB 10**"). On May 10, Mr. Mallet emailed me to confirm that he had received my email message and would get back to me as soon as possible. Because he had signed off by saying "Stay Safe.", I emailed him on May 11 to enquire if he had been signing off with "stay safe" for years or only since the "pandemic" started. On May 13, I emailed Mr. Mallet to enquire when I can expect a response from him. In that message, I suggested that begging God's forgiveness would be a logical first step for his client. To help him understand the root causes of the present dispute, I reminded him that – shortly before his assassination – JFK had warned the world that there was a plot underway to enslave every man, woman, and child on this planet, and that JFK had intended to expose this plot. I also included three memes that summarize the plot to which JFK was likely referring: 1) a meme that includes Saul Alinksy's plan for converting free societies into socialist/communist dictatorships, 2) two memes from an interview that Yuri Bezmenov (a former KGB agent who defected to the United States) gave in 1984 in which he warned the free world about the dangers of communism. On May 25, I received a letter from Mr. Mallet in which he stated that our discussion was over.

18) On April 23, 2021, I received a letter that was written with prejudice by counsel for the Wolfville Animal Hospital (Mr. Peter Nathanson of Nathanson Seaman Watts)

that contained at least one false statement: "We would also point out that your obvious inclination to pursue a political agenda against masking will, if pursued, have real implications for real people." ("**TAB 11**")

19) When counsel for the Wolfville Animal Hospital did not respond to the email messages I had sent him in response to his letter, I decided to send him a formal letter on April 30, 2021, in which I demonstrated why the statement I cited in the previous paragraph is false ("**TAB 12**"). I went on to explain to him that, rather than me pursuing a political agenda, I am fighting a political agenda and highlighted that the issue of concern for me in this dispute is that health care workers are requiring people to put their health at risk in order to have access to a health care service. I also highlighted that a prophecy in the Bible (Book of Revelation) is that there will come a time when all that is good will be perceived as evil and that all that is evil will be perceived as good, and that he could see evidence for this prophecy having been fulfilled by opening his eyes.

20) On May 4, 2021, I sent a follow-up letter to counsel for the Wolfville Animal Hospital with the hope that I could meet with him and his client to find a resolution that would involve us not having to go to court ("**TAB 13**"). In this letter, I pointed out to counsel that the Canadian Veterinary Oath states in part that veterinarians have promised to "protect the health of the public" and that the Provincial Dental Board of Nova Scotia's Code of Ethics requires dentists to "provide

for care to all members of society" (Article 5; Provision of Care) and to "protect the health of the patients" (Article 6; Delegation of Duties). I also pointed out to him that all he had to do was go to the Nova Scotia Barristers' Society's (NSBS) web page to see firsthand that the legal profession in Nova Scotia is not of sound mind (e.g., the web page contains a statement about "systemic racism" in Canada, the web page makes it clear that NSBS believes that the Truth and Reconciliation Commission's Report is a credible source of information, etc.). I also provided counsel for the Wolfville Animal Hospital with resources that speak to my credibility when it comes to the issue of me speaking truth. Finally, I proposed that this dispute could be resolved by him representing the Wolfville Animal Hospital and the other party for free, in exchange for neither party submitting a complaint to NSBS for the professional incompetence that he exhibited in his letter to me dated April 27, 2021. This paragraph demonstrates the fact that I did everything humanly possible to avoid taking Mr. Nathanson's client to court and that he is being dishonest when his firm's web site states that the lawyers at this firm "look for ways to resolve a dispute in a fair and reasonable manner before it gets to court".

21) On May 19, 2021, I submitted my Notice of Action and Statement of Claim to the Supreme Court of Nova Scotia. To these documents, I attached a letter in which I asked the court to process this proceeding as an urgent matter because it had implications for a free society. Had the court granted my

request, this matter could have been resolved in or around June and citizens would have been able to get their lives back on track. Unfortunately, my requests have been ignored or denied. It is blatantly obvious – as a point of fact – that the courts in Nova Scotia view the people that appear before them with contempt (especially if they are not represented by a lawyer), as exemplified by the recent announcement that mandatory vaccination policies do not apply to the judiciary ("**TAB 14**").

22) Because I have been accused of pursuing a political agenda, I am including a copy of the Vaccine Death Report that was published by Mr. David John Sorenson and Dr. Vladmir Zelenko in September 2021 ("**TAB 15**"). A point of fact worth highlighting is that the report reveals "the real risk of an unprecedented genocide".

23) Given the fact that this court has blood on its hands and given the fact that this court has been complicit with fraud, the only way for the court to redeem itself is to not only order the provincial government to overturn the Health Protection Act order immediately because it is unconstitutional (as well as to grant all of the other items in my Notice of Motion), but to also issue an apology to the public and – most importantly – to beg for God's forgiveness. A point of fact is that the court sessions start with a prothonotary declaring "God Save the Queen". At this stage, it is a fact that only God can save her and this court.

Sworn to before me	)
on ____________________, 2021	)
at Kentville, NS.	)

____

Rakesh ("Rick") Mehta, PhD

Index of Supporting Documents[19]

Mehta v. Wolfville Animal Hospital & Dr. Carrie Terry Family Dentistry Inc. (2021)
Ken No. 506242

TAB 1 Canadian Veterinary Oath.

TAB 2 Provincial Dental Board of Nova Scotia's Code of Ethics.

TAB 3 Rancourt, D. (April 2020). Masks Don't Work: A Review of Science Relevant to COVID-19 Social Policy. (Research Article)

TAB 4 Carpay, J. (July 25, 2020). Making Face Masks Mandatory is Not Backed by Science or Law. (Article published by the Post Millenial)

TAB 5 Archbishop Viganò's Open Letter to POTUS Donald J. Trump (October 25, 2020)

TAB 6 Letter from R. Mehta to Wolfville Animal Hospital (October 23, 2020)

TAB 7 Letter from Wolfville Animal Hospital to R. Mehta (October 27, 2020)

TAB 8 Email message from R. Mehta to Dr. Carrie Terry Family Dentistry Inc.; response from Dr. Terry's secretary; response from R. Mehta (February 3, 2021)

19 These documents were included with the affidavit that I swore to at the courthouse in Kentville, Nova Scotia, but are not being included in this book.

TAB 9 Email message from R. Mehta to Dr. Carrie Terry Family Dentistry Inc. and response (April 8, 2021)

Attached: Dismissal Letter

TAB 10 Email message from R. Mehta to Mr. G. Mallet (Sedgwick Canada Inc.) (May 7, 2021); response: May 10, 2021; follow-up messages by R. Mehta (May 11 and May 13, 2021)

Attached: 1) 1 meme that summarizes Saul Alinsky's plan
2) 2 memes from interview with Yuri Bezmenov

TAB 11 Letter from Mr. P. Nathanson (Counsel, Wolfville Animal Hospital) to R. Mehta (April 27, 2021)

TAB 12 Letter from R. Mehta to Mr. P. Nathanson (Counsel, Wolfville Animal Hospital) (April 30, 2021)

TAB 13 Letter from R. Mehta to Mr. P. Nathanson (Counsel, Wolfville Animal Hospital) (May 4, 2021)

TAB 14 Rankin. A. (November 25, 2021). Workplace Vaccine Policy Doesn't Apply to Nova Scotia Judges. (Article published by Saltwire)

TAB 15 Sorenson, D.J, & Zelenko, V. (September 2021). The Vaccine Death Report.

TAB 3: BODY OF LETTER TO THE CROWN'S OFFICE
(March 8, 2022)

1535 Meghan Drive
Coldbrook, NS
B4R 1A1

March 8, 2022

Kentville Crown Attorney's Office & Office of Chief Crown
49 Cornwallis Street, Suite 205
Kentville, NS
B4N 2E3

To Whom It May Concern:

According to Article 8 of the *Universal Declaration of Human Rights* that was passed by the United Nations, "Everyone has the right to an effective remedy by the competent national [and presumably provincial] tribunals for acts violating the fundamental rights granted him by the constitution or by law". The key word that I emphasize is the word "competent".

In addition, Section 15(1) of the Canadian Charter of Rights and Freedoms states: "Every individual is equal before and under the law and has the right to the equal protection and equal benefit of the law without discrimination and, in particular, without discrimination based on race, national or ethnic origin, colour, religion, sex, age or mental or physical disability."

I am writing to you because the Supreme Court of Nova Scotia has recently demonstrated that it is incompetent by discriminating against me for not being mentally disabled. To substantiate my concern, I have attached a copy of a recent decision by Justice Hunt regarding my constitutional challenge of the Health Protection Act order (the document labelled "A") and my response to his decision, which consists of the last email message that I sent to the Supreme Court of Nova Scotia (the document labelled "B") and a copy of the body of the letter that I sent to the Minister of Justice (the document labelled "C").

Please keep in mind that what happened to me was not an isolated incident; on May 14, 2021, Justice Norton approved an injunction order (Hfx. No. 506040) in which he failed to rule out conflict of interest on the part of Dr. Strang, i.e., an unelected bureaucrat.

I hope that you have a protocol in place for times in which the judiciary is insane, i.e., mentally unfit to serve the public's interests. In the event that you do not have a protocol in place for this type of situation, I would be happy to offer my services for free in order to help solve this problem. In order to establish my credibility, I will state that that my expertise is the understanding of human nature and that the mainstream media hates me. If you wish to reach me by phone, my landline number is 902-678-5876; I can also be reached by email at rick.mehta@hotmail.com.

I look forward to hearing back from you soon.

Sincerely,

Rakesh ("Rick") Mehta, PhD

TAB 4: COVER LETTER OF BRIEF SUBMITTED TO THE RCMP

(May 2, 2022)

1535 Meghan Drive
Coldbrook, NS
B4R 1A1

May 2, 2022

Royal Canadian Mounted Police (RCMP)
8833 Commercial Street
New Minas, NS
B4N 3C4

Dear RCMP New Minas Detachment:

Because I am not sure whether I should be addressing this brief to the RCMP or to the Halifax Regional Municipality (HRM) Police, I am hand-delivering one copy of this brief to the New Minas detachment of the RCMP because this detachment is in my neighborhood and I am mailing one copy of this brief to the HRM Police.

I ask that the person who is receiving this brief forward it to an investigator in the police department who specializes in organized crime. I also ask that the investigating officer reach out to me to confirm that they have received it; my contact information is on page 3 of this brief.

I am writing to you because I have caught Acadia University in a corruption scandal that involves, among other people, individuals in the Prime Minister's Office (including the Prime Minster himself), individuals within the judiciary in Nova Scotia, and individuals in the Nova Scotia Barristers' Society. For this reason, I request that criminal charges be laid against the following 34 individuals (listed in alphabetical order by surname):

1) Justice Joshua Arnold, Supreme Court of Nova Scotia
2) Peter Barnacle, General Counsel, Canadian Association of University Teachers
3) Andrew Biro, President, Acadia University Faculty Association
4) Scott Brison, Vice-Chair of Investment and Corporate Banking, Bank of Montreal, and Chancellor, Dalhousie University
5) Jonathan Cuming, TMC Law, Counsel retained by the Government of Nova Scotia and Dr. Carrie Family Dentistry Inc.
6) Elaine Cumming, Acting Director of Professional Responsibility, Nova Scotia Barristers' Society
7) Corinne Currie, Prothonotary, Kentville Justice Centre
8) George R.H. Franklin, Commissioner of Oaths or Barrister and Solicitor for the Province of Nova Scotia
9) Justice Timothy Gabriel, Supreme Court of Nova Scotia
10) Jack Graham, Counsel retained by Acadia University, Firm: McInnes Cooper
11) Adam Harris, Counsel retained by R. Mehta, Firm: Burchell MacDougall
12) Francesca Holyoke, Head of Archives and Special Collections, University of New Brunswick
13) Justice Jeffrey Hunt, Supreme Court of Nova Scotia

14) Raymond Ivany, Board of Directors, Bank of Canada
15) Arbitrator William Kaplan, Lawyer and Solicitor Based in Toronto who Received Direction and Payment from Acadia University and the Acadia University Faculty Association
16) Richard Karsten, Former President, Acadia University Faculty Association
17) Heidi Kimball, Counsel retained by R. Vermeiren, Firm: Kimball Law
18) Howard Levitt, Counsel (pro bono) retained by R. Mehta, Firm: Levitt Sheikh
19) Katrin MacPhee, Counsel retained by Acadia University Faculty Association, Firm: Pink Larkin
20) Barry Mason, Counsel retained by R. Mehta, Firm: Pressé Mason
21) Geoff Muttart, Counsel retained by R. Mehta, Firm: muttarts law
22) Peter Nathanson, NSW, Counsel retained by the Government of Nova Scotia and Wolfville Animal Hospital
23) Justice Scott Norton, Supreme Court of Nova Scotia
24) Anthony Pash, Former President, Acadia University Faculty Association
25) Erin Patterson, Former President, Acadia University Faculty Association
26) Melissa Pike, Counsel retained by Acadia University, Firm: McInnes Cooper
27) Ronald Pink, Counsel retained by Acadia University Faculty Association, Firm: Pink Larkin
28) Peter Ricketts, President and Vice Chancellor, Acadia University
29) Edwin Rosenberg, MD, FRCP(C)
30) Justice Ann Smith, Supreme Court of Nova Scotia

31) Penni Stewart, Associate Professor, York University
32) Prime Minister Justin Trudeau
33) Justice Gregory Warner, Supreme Court of Nova Scotia
34) N. Welch, Deputy Prothonotary, Kentville Justice Centre

The sections of the Criminal Code of Canada that I believe to be most directly relevant are perjury, fabricating evidence, and obstructing justice, which I cite below:

1) Perjury: "131 (1) Subject to subsection (3), every one commits perjury who, with intent to mislead, makes before a person who is authorized by law to permit it to be made before him a false statement under oath or solemn affirmation, by affidavit, solemn declaration or deposition or orally, knowing that the statement is false."

2) Fabricating evidence (section 137): "Every one who, with intent to mislead, fabricates anything with intent that it shall be used as evidence in a judicial proceeding, existing or proposed, by any means other than perjury or incitement to perjury is guilty of an indictable offence and liable to imprisonment for a term not exceeding fourteen years."

3) Obstructing justice: "139 (1) Every one who wilfully attempts in any manner to obstruct, pervert or defeat the course of justice in a judicial proceeding,
   (a) by indemnifying or agreeing to indemnify a surety, in any way and either in whole or in part, or

(b) where he is a surety, by accepting or agreeing to accept a fee or any form of indemnity whether in whole or in part from or in respect of a person who is released or is to be released from custody,

is guilty of

(a) an indictable offence and is liable to imprisonment for a term not exceeding two years, or
(b) an offence punishable on summary conviction.

I am trusting you to review this brief in its entirety and in good faith; in other words, I am trusting you to review not only the body of this brief, but also the evidence that I have included and the other sources that I have cited, e.g., videos of lectures. As well, I am trusting that you will ask me for clarification if you have questions about what I have written and that you will enforce other sections of the Criminal Code when it is clear that those sections have also been violated.

In the sections that follow, I will first submit to you the proverbial smoking gun that demonstrates beyond all doubt that the Criminal Code has been violated. I will then submit to you a comprehensive – yet concise – summary of the major events that led to this submission so that you can make an informed decision as you decide which charges apply to each individual that needs to be brought to justice. Because facts do not exist in a vacuum, I will cite other sources where relevant in order to help you to understand the context in which the facts occurred. Because this brief is information-dense, I recommend that you review the evidence that I cite as you read each numbered paragraph in this brief.

I realize that this brief is lengthy, but if I have done my job effectively it should read like a novel about a geeky academic who is forced to play the roles of detective and lawyer when he finds himself in a web of deceit involving organized crime and politics.

Respectfully submitted,

Rakesh ("Rick") Mehta, PhD
Former Professor, Acadia University
Currently: Owner, Grassroots Health Foods Ltd.
Telephone: Home: (902) 678-5876, Cell: (902) 670-5876, Work: (902) 681-2169
Email: rick.mehta@hotmail.com

CC: Halifax Regional Municipality Police Department

TAB 5: BODY OF LETTER TO CONSTABLE BELLINGHAM

(May 4, 2022)

1535 Meghan Drive
Coldbrook, NS
B4R 1A1

May 4, 2022

Royal Canadian Mounted Police (RCMP)
8833 Commercial Street
New Minas, NS
B4N 3C4

Dear Constable Bellingham:

Because I did not record the meeting that we had yesterday from 12 pm to 1 pm, I thought that I should write to you so that we have a record of what transpired during the meeting and my thoughts regarding the meeting.

1) As a point of fact, I spent close to one month putting together my brief. In contrast, you phoned me roughly 24 hours after I had submitted my brief to your detachment and asked to meet with me. If I was a police officer and I was asking to meet with a member of the public who had come forward with information regarding a large scale organized crime syndicate, I would have first done my homework on that person so that I could assess the extent

to which that person is credible, e.g., check that person's social media posts, read the hit pieces that have been published about him by Canada's fake news media, watch whatever videos are online that feature that person, etc.

Had you done your homework (e.g., by knowing every detail of my brief backward and forward before asking to meet with me), you would have known that the last research presentation that I did while I was a tenured professor was titled "[The Relationship Between Political Orientation and] Bullshit Detection in Canadian Politics" and understood that my background would make me an expert witness who can bring down our governments because I can speak to the bigger issues that affect our society, e.g., breach of trust on the part of our politicians, law societies, and courts. Worded somewhat differently, I am among the people that the establishment fears because of what I know, i.e., knowledge is power.

2) In part because my background is in psychology and in part because I spent my academic career teaching students how to think instead of what to think, I found it interesting that you accused me of not thinking logically. To counter your claim, I have attached a copy of an article recently published by Dr. Kenneth Westhues (Professor Emeritus, Sociology and Legal Studies, University of Waterloo) in which he provides an updated analysis on the case of Dr. Denis Rancourt (Former

Professor, University of Ottawa); interestingly, I cited Dr. Rancount in paragraph 44 of my brief and included a copy of one of his articles in TAB 40 of my brief.

3) When I explained the importance of people responding with "I comprehend" instead of "I understand" after an officer who is abusing his or her power has read people their rights while arresting them, you responded by saying that I was being nitpicky with words. This comment concerns me because it tells me that you do not understand that language is connected to thought or the importance of people being precise with their language given that words have meaning.

4) Related to the issue of thinking clearly, I recall you stating words to the effect that there may actually be a rationale for people to wear face diapers. If you believe that breathing your body's waste products is going to protect anyone from the world's deadliest disease or that we ever were in the midst of a pandemic – especially after reading the body of my brief and the articles that I included in TABS 40 and 41 – that would be consistent with the adage that it is far easier to fool people than to convince them that they have been fooled.

5) I noted that I saw little evidence of you being able to discern facts vs. opinions, truth vs lies, who is acting in good faith vs. bad faith (abuse of power), etc. This concerns me because you are in a position

of authority whereas I am not. As Voltaire once noted, those that can be made to believe absurdities can also be made to commit atrocities; see also: Christopher R. Browning's "Ordinary Men: Reserve Police Battalion 101 and the Final Solution in Poland".

6) I observed that you lost your composure during the meeting whereas I did not lose my composure. While you were accusing me of being rude, I thought to myself that your comment was in line with that of Joseph Goebbels (Minister of Propaganda for the Nazi party): "Accuse the other side of that which you are guilty".

I will close by saying that what I observed in yesterday's meeting was consistent with what Yuri Bezmenov (ex-KGB agent who defected to the US) said in an interview back in 1984 regarding the effectiveness of the brainwashing techniques that were used in communist Russia and in which he warned the free world of what to expect in the future unless communism was weeded out:

> "They are contaminated; they are programmed to think and to react to certain stimuli in a certain pattern. You cannot change their minds, even if you expose them to authentic information, even if you prove that black is black and white is white, you still cannot change the basic perception and the logic of behaviour. In other words, the process of demoralization is complete and irreversible".

Fast forward to the present, the new name for communism is "social justice" (same pig, different shade of lipstick). And since the outset of COVID, I have stated repeatedly on social media that the problem of our time is not a lack of information but the fact that people have lost the ability to think.

I will leave it to you to decide how you wish to proceed in light of this letter; the ideal outcome may be that you pass on my brief to Police on Guard for Thee.

Sincerely,

Rick Mehta, PhD
Defender of Truth ("I am the way, the truth, and the life" -- Jesus Christ, John 14:6; KJV)

TAB 6: BODY OF LETTER TO THE CROWN'S OFFICE
(June 3, 2022)

1535 Meghan Drive
Coldbrook, NS
B4R 1A1

June 3, 2022

Kentville Crown Attorney's Office & Office of Chief Crown
49 Cornwallis Street, Suite 205
Kentville, NS
B4N 2E3

Dear Crown Attorneys:

Enclosed with this letter are 3 documents that I list below in reverse chronological order:

1) The first of three letters that I submitted to Constable Bellingham (RCMP, New Minas Detachment). This one is dated May 4, 2022.
    a. Please note that I have not heard from Constable Bellingham since I met with her on May 3, 2022. Given that it has been a month since I have heard from her, the next logical step for me was to reach out to your office.
2) The body of a brief that I submitted to the RCMP New Minas Detachment on May 2, 2022.[20]

20 The RCMP has a signed copy of my brief that contains a hard copy of the supporting documents that I cited in the body of my

3) The body of a letter that I mailed to both your office and the RCMP New Minas Detachment on March 8, 2022.[21]

To date, I have not received a response from either your office or the RCMP to my letter dated March 8, 2022, or a response to any of three letters that I submitted to Constable Bellingham, which I interpret as evidence that both divisions of law enforcement are indifferent to the fact that the judiciary in Nova Scotia is insane (i.e., mentally unfit to serve the public's interests) and therefore condone this disservice to Canadians.

Because I am a psychologist whose expertise is in judgment and decision making – and who also happens to be a Christian – I am in a position to provide you with a professional opinion regarding the irrational conduct that I have observed from both your office and the RCMP in response to COVID-19: We are living in an age of mass psychosis – an epidemic of madness (mental illness) in which a large portion of the population has lost touch with reality – that is being caused by large scale demonic possession courtesy of Satan. From a legal perspective, Satan's demons have violated not only the "supremacy of God" that both the *Canadian Charter of Rights and Freedoms* and *Canadian Bill of Rights* cite as a prerequisite to "rule of law" in a free society, but also Canada's *Criminal Code* by causing those whom they have possessed to be complicit with the largest *fraud* scheme in the history of humanity.

---

brief. I respectfully request that the RCMP and your office treat my brief as if it was a police report that was submitted by an undercover officer.

21 Your office already has a signed copy of this letter and a hard copy of the supporting documents that I cited in this letter.

The good news is that I have discovered a cure for this highly unusual state of affairs. Based on my understanding of the Bible, I hypothesize that this problem can be solved if at least one Crown Attorney takes me up on my offer to give them a spanking on their bottom until that person has come to their senses; I emphasize that the spanking will be given to the person after I have prayed for them and I assure you that the spanking will be given with love instead of hate, anger, or vengeance. Once that person has come to their senses, he or she will be in a position to understand the brief that I have enclosed and to then take steps to ensure that justice is served to the people to whom I am making the following additional charge: *Obstruction of Justice by Abusing the Process of the Court.*

The rationale for the treatment that I have developed is that the Bible has directed Christians to be shrewd as serpents yet gentle as doves as they try to save as many souls as possible before Judgement Day arrives (i.e., the day is fast approaching that God is going to judge the living and the dead); the Bible also calls on Christians to lay hands on the sick so that the sick can be healed. To accomplish my goal of healing the sick by giving them a spanking on their bottom, I will first pray for the Holy Spirit to ensure that my spanking will evict the demonic spirit that is living inside that person and that the Holy Spirit will then replace that person's heart of stone with a heart of flesh and will also replace the demonic spirit that is currently living inside that person with a new spirit so that Christ will live in that person instead of the demonic spirit. In short, the free service I am offering in my capacity as a Christian whose expertise is the understanding of human nature is salvation through spiritual rebirth courtesy of the Holy Trinity (Father, Son, and Holy Spirit). Think of it as a "Great Reset".

I hope that your office will "trust the science" and take me up on my offer – if not for yourselves, then for the sake of the accused who need to be saved. With regard to a spanking protocol that needs to be negotiated, I recommend that the spanking be done under Constable Bellingham's supervision and that other officers take care of hosting, as well as recording and/or livestreaming the event; we also need to negotiate other details such as which media outlets should be invited to this event, catering for the post-spanking reception, etc.

While your office is more than welcome to ignore or refuse my offer, I warn you that it would be a foolish move on your part to ignore Biblical prophecy regarding the second coming of Christ; if I was in your shoes, I would be embarrassed at the thought of having to spend the rest of eternity in hell when our Father asks you: "Why didn't you take Dr. Mehta up on his kind and generous offer? It's not as if he offered to nail you to a cross to pay the price for someone else's burden."

I therefore hope that you will choose wisely and that I will hear back from you soon.

Sincerely,

Rakesh ("Rick") Mehta, PhD
Former Professor, Acadia University
Defender of Truth ("I am the way, the truth, and the life" - Jesus Christ, John 14:6; KJV)

1) CC (hard copy of letter only): Constable Bellingham, RCMP, New Minas Detachment

2) CC (via email only and only if I have the person's email address): The 34 individuals I have named in the cover letter of my brief

TAB 7: EMAIL MESSAGE TO MEMBERS OF WESTON CHRISTIAN FELLOWSHIP
(July 10, 2022)

From: Rick Mehta

Date: Sun 2022-07-10 8:51 PM

To: Names Not Being Disclosed

Subject: ICYI: Copy of Comment on Church's Facebook Page

According to the web site: "Christina Lazier is the top-notch lawyer working hard for Weston Christian Fellowship and she says she is launching a Charter challenge of the police actions against the church."

The complication, though, is that Canadians don't have any rights under the Charter. If you don't believe me, look at the Charter and you'll notice that it first states that there are "reasonable limits" to our rights and freedoms before disclosing to us our rights and freedoms.

Seems odd to me that this "top-notch lawyer" is "launching a Charter challenge" when another option available is the Canadian Bill of Rights, which was signed by PM Diefenbaker and was written in the spirit of the FREE society that our soldiers fought and died for in WW2; this is in contrast to the spirit of the JUST society that Pierre Elliott Trudeau imposed onto Canadians without their informed consent. The Charter in turn paved the way for Justin Trudeau's "SOCIAL JUSTICE" policies; please note that the word "justice" becomes corrupted when a qualifier is placed in front of it and that there are no references to "social justice" in the Bible.

One doesn't need a law degree to figure this out; common sense is enough. However, as the saying goes, common sense is not so common -- thanks in large part to Canada's education system, which is worse than useless, i.e., it kills common sense.

A point of fact is that Lazier is a product of Canada's "education" system. Another point of fact is that I cannot find any public statements by her in which she is critical of our education system or of the law society to which she belongs (NSBS) that bases its policies on principles of social justice, e.g., NSBS treats the Truth and Reconciliation Commission's Report as credible even though its findings are based on a biased sample of people who were asked leading questions.

In contrast, my record as an advocate for truth speaks for itself.

IMHO: With friends like Lazier, this church doesn't need enemies. A further complication is that my impression is that the leaders appear to be clueless about notions such as "wolves in sheep's clothing" or false prophets (whether these people became wolves or false prophets by choice or by circumstance is a different issue).

If what I have just stated is fact instead of just an opinion, then this demonstrates a psychological phenomenon known as the Kruger-Dunning Effect on the part of Lazier and/or the church leaders -which refers to being clueless about one's own cluelessness - or as Gad Saad defines it in "The Parasitic Mind: How Infectious

Ideas are Killing Common Sense": "a self-assuredness and supreme confidence despite one's idiocy."

Lord help them for they know not what they are doing.

If my language seems harsh, I am trying to shake people out of their stupor. And if I am proven wrong, then I will not only delete this comment but also make a public apology for this post.

My post is motivated by this quotation by Thomas Sowell (arguably one of the most brilliant minds of our time, imho): "When you want to help people, you tell them the truth. When you want to help yourself, you tell them what they want to hear."

I hope that the church leaders will agree that a disruption in the church that is based in truth is more important than harmony that is based on a lie.

What are your thoughts?

TAB 8: LETTER TO KENTVILLE JUSTICE CENTRE
(July 25, 2022)

1535 Meghan Drive
Coldbrook, NS
B4R 1A1

July 25, 2022

Kentville Justice Centre
87 Cornwallis Street
Kentville, NS
B4N 2E5

RE: KEN No.: 8513762, 8513748, 8513749

Dear Kentville Justice Centre:

When I was a member of the Weston Christian Fellowship Church, I came across a copy of a court document that was left behind in the room in which the congregation gathers for lunch after the sermons on Sundays: "Notice of Intention to Raise Constitutional Argument" (June 24, 2022).

When I reviewed the document, I was quite shocked by what I had read. Rather than do a point-by-point critique, I will raise two issues that came to mind that made me question Rebel News' claim (October 20, 2021) that the church is receiving legal representation from a "top-notch lawyer":

1) On page 9, I noticed the lawyer cited the *English Standard Version* of the Bible instead of the *King James Version* of the Bible. This suggests to me that both the clients and lawyer are unaware of the historical significance of the *King James Version* of the Bible, i.e., that this is the version of the Bible – which dates back to 1611 and is often known as the Authorized version of the Bible – that people swear to in courtrooms in free societies.

2) On page 10, paragraph 25 states that "A paper copy of the Injunction granted by Justice Norton of the Supreme Court of Nova Scotia was served in person on Elder Meadows by the RCMP". Much to my surprise, unless I am mistaken in my understanding, it appears that the "top-notch lawyer" is oblivious to the fact that Justice Norton failed to rule out conflict of interest on the part of Dr. Strang when he granted the Injunction.

The other reason that I am writing to you is to provide you with information about the content of character in the church's leadership. On or about Tuesday, July 19, a member of the church (Glen Harnish) posted the following comment on my wall on Facebook: "This message is from one of the elders (Mike [Slauenwhite]). He doesn't use Facebook, but wanted to share some words with you Rick….". I found this statement odd because it took me only a few seconds to find Elder Slauenwhite's Facebook profile. If you or anyone else disagrees with my assessment that Elder Slauenwhite is a liar, I would be very much interested in knowing their reasons for disagreeing with me.

The only comment I will make is that Jesus Christ warns us about the consequences of the blind leading the blind: Both end up in a ditch. All I know is that I am grateful for having been evicted by a church that – in my professional and personal opinion – is being led by wolves in sheep's clothing.

Please feel free to reach out to me if you have any questions or concerns.

Sincerely,

Rakesh ("Rick") Mehta, PhD
Cognitive Psychologist & Defender of Truth
Email: rick.mehta@hotmail.com
Telephone: (902) 670-5876

CC: Marty Elson, Weston Christian Fellowship Church (3 copies: 1 for Elson, 1 for church, and 1 for church's counsel)

Kentville Crown Attorney's Office & Office of Chief Crown (1 copy for the Queen's counsel)

TAB 9: EMAIL MESSAGE TO CPL. TREMBLAY
(December 7, 2022)

From: Rick Mehta

Date: Wed 2022-12-07 6:55 PM

To: Email Address Not Being Disclosed

Subject: Question About Your Signature

Dear Cpl. Tremblay,

I noticed that there is a dash in your signature (i.e., "Royal Canadian Mounted Police—Government of Canada"); a point of fact that I wish to highlight is that the dash is in a place where a reasonable person would not expect to see a dash, i.e., between the words "Police" and "Government." For example, a dash makes sense in the context of a "scientist-practitioner" because it implies that the practitioner is basing their treatments on science, but it does not make sense in the context of a police organization that claims on its website to have the ability to do "Federal and International Operations" in a manner that serves only the public's/taxpayer's interests.

Unless the RCMP can prove in a court of law that they were acting in the public's interests, as opposed to the Government of Canada's interests, when they arrested and charged Ms. Morgan May Guptill and Mr. Jeremy MacKenzie, then I believe that it's clear that the only conclusion that can be derived is that these arrests were motivated by politics instead of a duty to serve the public's interests.

Given the evidence, I hope that you would agree that the charges against Ms. Guptill and Mr. MacKenzie should be dropped and that you will cooperate with me by forwarding this message to the relevant people in Nova Scotia and other parts of Canada so that my request can be processed.

Thank you for your time and attention to this matter.

Sincerely,

Rick Mehta, PhD
Cognitive Psychologist and Defender of Truth

TAB 10: EMAIL MESSAGE TO DARTMOUTH PROVINCIAL COURT
(December 13, 2022)

From: Rick Mehta

Date: Tue 2022-12-13 12: 13 PM

Attached: Mehta – Email Message to Cpl Tremblay Regarding Signature.pdf

To: Email Address Not Being Disclosed

Subject: Question about Provincial Court's Case against Morgan May Guptill and Jeremy MacKenzie

Dear Provincial Court (Dartmouth),

I am writing to you regarding the court's case against Ms. Morgan May Guptill and Mr. Jeremy MacKenzie, and am doing so in three capacities:

1) my capacity as a cognitive psychologist whose area of expertise is judgment and decision making,
2) my capacity as a concerned member of the public, and
3) my capacity as a Christian.

Attached is a copy of an email message that I sent to Cpl. Tremblay of the RCMP on December 7, 2022. I note that he did not respond to my message. I hope that we can agree that a reasonable interpretation for his lack of a response has to do with him not wishing to acknowledge that Ms. Guptill's and Mr. Mackenzie's arrests were motivated by politics instead of duty to serve the public's interests.

A key point that the court needs to understand is that we are living in age of postmodernism (the view that there is no objective truth), which in turn explains why we are living in an age of mass psychosis in which mental illness is the norm; unfortunately, the court has never been immune to this predicament.

A further complication that I have discovered is that the symptoms of psychosis (losing touch with reality) manifest themselves differently in people who have drank the COVID Kool-Aid versus people who have not drank the COVID Kool-Aid, which in turn makes the symptoms of psychosis harder to detect within the freedom movement.

The good news, though, is that – by the grace of God – I have developed a treatment for mass psychosis that is the spiritual equivalent of electro-convulsive therapy (ECT). In a nutshell, the treatment consists of me praying for the patient before giving that person their choice of a spanking on their bottom or kicks to their ass until they come to their senses; the treatment is to be later followed by a celebration of fellowship with friends, family, and former enemies who are now friends as all parties unite under Jesus Christ.

Even better news is that I am willing to provide this service for FREE to everyone involved with the Crown Attorney's case (including the officers who made the arrests and Cpl. Tremblay) and with the court – starting with the Chief Justice.

I hope that you will agree that I have come with a novel, forward-thinking, and cost-effective approach for reforming Canada's justice system so that our laws are more in line with God's law. If you have any questions or concerns, please let me know. Otherwise, I look forward to working with you so that we can prevent a travesty of justice. Specifically, I ask that you provide me with the information that I need so that I can put forward a motion for the court to dismiss the Crown Attorney's case against Ms. Guptill and Mr. MacKenzie.

Sincerely,

Rick Mehta, PhD
Cognitive Psychologist & Defender of Truth

Epilogue

In Section 1 of this book, I stated that the symptoms of mass psychosis are harder to detect in those who have not drank the COVID Kool-Aid than in those who have. I would like to elaborate on this point briefly here. Before I do, I will state that one major lesson I have learned in my lifetime is that all people have a need for spiritual fulfillment and that, for this reason, all people worship; in other words, the question we should be asking ourselves is "which god do you worship" instead of "do you worship a god?" A second major lesson that I have learned is that feeling good about oneself is the primary force that drives human nature and that most people will do whatever it takes to feel good about themselves, including going to great lengths to control other people if necessary.

Until June 2022, I had a social circle within the freedom movement. That changed after I had circulated a copy of my letter to the Crown Attorney's Office (dated June 3, 2022; TAB 6) to people who I had thought were my friends. Interestingly, the way in which my social circle related to me changed depending on their spiritual beliefs, but the end result was the same.

I eventually discovered that the people who were atheists wanted nothing to do with me because I talked openly about my faith in God. Based on their conduct, I have no choice but to conclude that atheists are a cult of people who not only believe adamantly that God does not exist, but who also outright reject any evidence that a believer in God would present to them that demonstrates that God not only exists, but is also making a difference in people's lives. From what I can tell, atheism is a mental illness that afflicts people regardless of their political orientation, i.e., conservatives and liberals are equally at risk for atheism.[22]

Among the people who have spiritual beliefs, I have noticed that all of them have unwittingly disclosed that they are postmodernists. For example, I have noticed that postmodernists often use the expression "speak your truth." This language does not surprise me when it is spoken by people who follow New Age philosophies that work on the premise that there is a universal God who will save everyone, regardless of whether they have morals or are immoral. Interestingly, these people also tend to talk excessively about energies, frequencies, and vibrations. My impression is that these people believe that there is a relationship between these physical phenomena and morality (e.g., that vibrating at the correct frequency, whatever that may be, will make an individual into a moral person); this belief is consistent with the worldview adopted by "tree huggers" and others who worship plants. Many of these people have also rejected me because I have talked openly about my faith in Jesus Christ.

I was shocked and taken aback, however, when a member of Weston Christian Fellowship (most likely a Christian conservative) exclaimed, "Speak your truth elsewhere" when he lost the debate that we were having.

22 **Editor's Note*:** Renowned Christian philosopher Alvin Plantinga sees atheism as a cognitive consequence of sin. See Alvin Plantinga, *Warranted Christian Belief* (New York: Oxford University Press, 2000). Similarly, Catholic philosopher, theologian, and counselor Fr. John J. Pasquini sees atheism as a personality disorder that can be traced back to childhood development. See Fr. John J. Pasquini, *Atheist Personality Disorder: Addressing A Distorted Mindset* (Bloomington: AuthorHouse, 2010).

I was taken aback by this response because I would have thought that Christians of all people would understand that there is only one objective truth and that that truth is Jesus Christ.

From what I can tell, Christians —at least the ones who live in my area—either subscribe to social justice ideology (which is based in part on postmodernism) and therefore attend woke churches, or they are Christian conservatives who are postmodernists; the latter group of people have much in common with conservatives who are atheists. In other words, most Christians seem to have more in common with atheists and followers of New Age philosophy than they may believe. I hope that the reader is asking themselves "Why might this be the case?"

Given that the Bible states that believers in Jesus Christ are the light of the world, if my suspicion that most Christians have conformed Jesus Christ to their image instead of conforming themselves to the image of Jesus Christ is correct, then the only logical conclusion that I can make is that most Christians delude themselves into thinking that they are worshipping Jesus Christ when in fact they are worshipping themselves. A point of fact that I will highlight is that worshipping oneself is synonymous with worshipping Satan. If my suspicion is based on fact, then it should also come as no surprise to the reader why this chapter of human history is so dark.

Rather than despair, followers of Jesus Christ should remove the plank that is in their eye before worrying about the speck of wood in someone else's eye. I say this not out of malice or spite, but to point out to other believers in Jesus Christ that it is impossible to save someone else's soul unless one's own moral and spiritual house is in order. Perhaps the best way for Christians to address this issue is by analyzing and repairing their spiritual home's foundation; I say this because the storm of our time is still in its earliest stages and is only going to get worse as Biblical prophecies in Revelation continue to materialize. There is much to do, and the clock is ticking. Let's get to work.

Manufactured by Amazon.ca
Bolton, ON

32502588R00072